T0194577

SPARED

TRUE STORIES OF FAMILY & FRIENDS

ALICE FAYE AND BRIANNA

authorHOUSE®

AuthorHouse™
1663 Liberty Drive
Bloomington, IN 47403
www.authorhouse.com
Phone: 1 (800) 839-8640

Published by AuthorHouse 03/11/2019

ISBN: 978-1-7283-0380-2 (sc)
ISBN: 978-1-7283-0379-6 (e)

Print information available on the last page.

This book is printed on acid-free paper.

CHAPTER 1

Some of these stories were so hard for me to write, it felt as if my heart would break into thousands of pieces.

My story begins with my daddy, who I simply called "Daddy" until later in my life. You will find out later in my story why I began to call him "Dad" instead. For now, though, I'll begin with my daddy's maternal grandparents, Great Grandpa and Great Grandma Dew. They lived in east Tennessee. They had a farm with pigs, horses, cows, and goats.

Now for my daddy's mother and father, Joe and Samantha. Grandpa and Grandma had three sons: my daddy, Jim, and his brothers, Lenny and Rick.

Grandma was becoming mentally ill when Daddy was a young boy; to her, everybody was Lenny. When my daddy was about six years old, she would sometimes take him to the hog pen on Great Grandpa Dew's farm and lock him in it to play house. She would go back to the farmhouse to bring him food but then forget about him for hours and hours.

Eventually, when he was in the third grade, Dad quit school to help Great Grandpa Dew work on the farm, and because of his mother's mental illness, my daddy ended up being raised by his grandpa Dew.

Grandpa was a mean man at times. He would give

Grandma boiling coffee to drink, just to watch her reaction as she tried to drink it. Grandpa would run around with other women in front of Grandma, knowing she wasn't capable of leaving him.

It wasn't only Grandma that he was mean to. He also took out his anger on his kids sometimes. When Uncle Rick got into any trouble, Grandpa would put him in a large potato sack and hold him over an open fire. The abuse caused Uncle Rick to leave home when he was still a teenager.

Like Grandma, my uncle Lenny was also mentally ill. Unfortunately, Lenny was not spared when it came to Grandpa's cruelty. When Uncle Lenny was a young boy, Grandpa would hit him on his head with sticks of firewood.

CHAPTER 2

Now, my mother's parents, Marthia and Roman, were a bit of a different story. They were also from the eastern parts of Tennessee, and they had seven children: Noel; Otis; Norman; Sut; Velma; my mother, Ellie; and Brock.

Grandpa Roman was a deputy sheriff in the county. There had been a time, though, when he was involved with a married woman named Marsha. One day Marsha's husband found out about the affair going on between his wife and my grandpa, and when he actually saw Grandpa and her together, he grabbed her and started beating her. Grandpa Roman tried to stop him to arrest him, but he resisted so much that Grandpa Roman had no choice but to shoot him. He died, and Grandpa Roman was tried for murder but found innocent. But his affair with Marsha caused his and Grandma's divorce.

Grandpa and Marsha moved to Ohio, leaving Grandma to take care of all the children. Mom was seven years old and going to a nearby school that Daddy had attended earlier. One day Mom and Aunt Velma were playing at home in their backyard, gathering small sticks for Aunt Velma to chop. When Aunt Velma ran out of sticks, she told Mom to put her finger on the chopping block for a stick. Mom did it, and Aunt

Velma chopped part of Mom's finger off. Aunt Velma was two years older than Mom.

Grandpa sent Grandma only $5.00 a month, so Grandma had to pick blackberries to sell to help buy food. Because of all the hard work Grandma was left to do, she asked the judge if he would have Grandpa take more responsibility for their children. Grandpa had no choice but to agree with the judge's decision to help. Instead of having to take all the children back to Ohio with him, he only had to take some of them. Mom was one of the children he took.

Grandpa and Marsha got married and used their home for a boardinghouse. Mom was still a very young child, but she had to help Marsha cook, clean, and do laundry for the boarders, which left very little time for Mom to do her homework. I'm glad Marsha loved Mom and they worked well together, which helped Mom manage as well as she did.

When Mom was fifteen, the hard work plus her schooling got the better of her, so she quit school after finishing the seventh grade.

Toward the end of 1941, Daddy was in World War II as an MP. He was released with an honorable discharge some years later. He had been married to a woman named Peg, and they had two daughters. Daddy and Peg got a divorce. One day Daddy visited a male friend who was staying in the boardinghouse. Mom was still working there with Marsha. When Daddy saw Mom, he just had to introduce himself, and they started dating. He asked her to move to Tennessee with him, and she did. After they settled in, they went to Georgia and got married and then went back to their home.

Mom's dream was that Daddy would be her knight in shining armor, that he would take her away from all her hard work, and that he would love, cherish, and honor her for the rest of her life. But her heart was broken, and her dreams shattered because they never came true. Daddy and Mom's worst marital problems began after she gave birth to my beautiful sister, Connie, in mid-1948 in Tennessee.

Grandma Marthia married Levi Crawley, who became my dearest grandpa. He and his first wife, Omayra, had seven children: Mindy and Ivan, who both died during infancy, and then there were Vance, Victor, Peter, CJ, and Rena. Mom and her siblings all got along well together except for their little fights and arguments, which didn't amount to much.

Grandpa and Grandma had two sons together: Roland and Jonathan. Uncle Roland, Aunt Brandie, and Uncle John played an important role in my life, for which I will always be grateful. You will find out as you read on.

CHAPTER 3

Daddy never was satisfied anywhere; he was like his dad—always moving. Although he had very little education, he always found work. His drinking caused him to be more abusive to Mom. He started drinking when he was a young boy; Mom never took up the habit. She said that when Daddy was married to Peg, he got drunk on one particular day and tried to run over Peg with his car while she was standing in her yard. Mom had no doubt that he was lying.

Mom left Daddy and hitchhiked across a mountain with Connie while pregnant with me. A man came along and gave them about a fifty-mile ride to Grandpa and Grandma Crawley's home. Daddy came up, and he and Mom got back together. They moved far into the woods in back of Grandpa and Grandma Crawley's home.

When Mom went into labor, Daddy had a neighbor lady stay with her while he went for the doctor. Then I was born at the beginning of 1950.

Daddy moved us to a city in middle Tennessee when I was ten months old. We lived in a two-story house. One day, Mom and Connie were upstairs while Mom was doing her housework; Connie crawled through the bottom of a broken glass pane and walked onto the small porch that didn't have rails.

Connie fell to the ground on top of a coal pile. It was a miracle that some of the sharp edges of the coal didn't puncture her. The fall knocked the breath out of her and bruised her quite a bit. Mom had to get a neighbor lady to rush her and Connie to the hospital because Daddy was too drunk to take them. The doctor told Mom that Connie's bones were so soft that it had kept every bone in her body from breaking.

CHAPTER 4

‎‏..

We moved to Florida into a two-story apartment upstairs.
The landlady lived downstairs.

One morning, Daddy told Mom to be ready at noon
because he was going to take her to the grocery store. Mom
didn't have much time to clean their apartment and get me,
Connie, and herself ready. She worked extra hard and as fast
as she could. Her last chore was cleaning the floors. She finally
finished scrubbing them on her hands and knees and then got
all of us dressed.

She waited and waited for Daddy. When he finally came
home, it was late, with not much daylight left, and he was
drunk. Mom asked him if he was still going to take her to the
grocery store. Daddy got mad and started beating on her. She
was shocked and terrified. She managed to get away from him
and ran out of their apartment and down the long hallway.
By the time she reached the stairs, Daddy caught up with her
and kicked her down the flight of stairs. She was eight months
pregnant at the time.

The landlady came out of her apartment to see what all
the noise was about. She saw Mom on the floor with Daddy
still beating on her. She got ahold of Mom, pulled her inside

her apartment, and told Daddy if he didn't leave Mom alone, she was going to call the law on him. He left.

Mom was nervous and shook up. It took the landlady a long time to help Mom calm down and pull herself together. I thank the Lord that Mom didn't lose my brother. He was born in the spring of 1952; they named him Caleb.

CHAPTER 5

Daddy moved us back to Tennessee; he took us to visit Great-Grandpa and Grandma Dew, as we had many times before. I loved Great-Grandma Dew's chocolate cakes—they were the best. I also loved animals, so Great-Grandpa Dew gave me one of his goats. While visiting Great-Grandpa Dew, I was going outside to play with my goat, and I saw Great-Grandpa Dew shoot it. I started crying as I ran to tell Mom. I didn't understand that we had to have it for food until it was explained to me, but it broke my heart just the same.

Great-Grandpa Dew knew I loved to dance, so he would pay me a nickel to tap dance for him while he played his banjo. Dancing for Great-Grandpa is one of my fondest memories; I felt like I was on cloud nine. I thought that I was just like Shirley Temple—although I was far from it! Great-Grandma Dew paid me a dime to help her clean her house. They knew I would have done it for nothing, but they enjoyed paying me.

Mom became very ill. She went to the doctor and was diagnosed with tuberculosis. She was very weak and frail. It was a hard struggle for her to pack the things she needed for her stay in the hospital. It was even harder for her to take a bus to a city in the southeast part of the Tennessee, where the hospital was, which she had to do because Daddy was drunk and refused to take her.

Daddy moved to Ohio and had the hospital transfer Mom there. Altogether, she stayed in the hospital a year. We siblings stayed with different babysitters. After Mom was discharged, she got pregnant, and in the summer of 1955, my brother Derrick was born.

Later that year, our town flooded, which was scary and didn't turn out well for me. When Mom and Daddy carried us through the floodwater to safety, I got soaked. I wound up getting pneumonia, and I had to be admitted into the hospital where a sweet nurse gave me my first doll. It was a Tiny Tears doll, which became my traveling companion for years after. So, it all turned out all right. After being discharged from the hospital, we lived in a one-bedroom trailer. Grandpa and Grandma lived nearby.

One day Grandpa was babysitting me, Connie, and Caleb while Daddy and Mom took Derrick with them to go shopping. Caleb and I tried to play with some ducks that were swimming nearby, but they wouldn't be still, so Grandpa told us to go to the trailer and bring back some bread, keep it in our hands, and be real still. He said that when the ducks came to eat, we should grab them by their necks. That's what we did. Every time we caught one, we put it in our bedroom. We did this until the bedroom was full of ducks.

Caleb and I were having a ball playing with our new feathered friends. At least, until Mom and Daddy came home. They didn't like our idea of fun, so Mom took a broom and ran our friends out of our home. Caleb and I weren't happy about it because we had to watch all our hard work fly away! Mom wasn't happy with us because she had to clean up the mess; meanwhile, Daddy fussed at Grandpa for letting us do it to begin with.

My grandpa was all for making sure that we always had things to play with or something to do. Sometimes he would take us down to the dump to scavenge toys that had been thrown away. Once we found all we could, we would take them home and my mom would clean them up or fix them however she could for us. It was a poor life at times, but we did what we had to do. Besides, as children, we really didn't realize how poor we were; we just knew we were getting new-to-us toys that we worked hard to find—with Grandpa's help, of course. I'll always remember those special times with Grandpa and those special little things that he did for us!

CHAPTER 6

We moved to central Florida into a two-story house that stood on pilings. The floor was hardwood, which made it easy for Caleb to ride his tricycle. We had an outhouse in the back yard, and the yard was full of sandburs—imagine tiny green and brown sea urchins sticking to the soles of your feet! When we were young children, most of our homes had outhouses. When we lived in homes with inside bathrooms, I felt rich. Anyway, our yard had sandburs. Mom tried to get us kids to wear our shoes when we played outside, but we would forget and get those spiny sandburs in our feet. Mom had to carry us into our home and pick them out. Everything she did, she did out of pure motherly love for us. There's a song that says, "If there's medals for mothers, Momma, you'd win everyone." That's how I truly feel about my precious mother, but until I grew into my middle teens, I just thought of her as an unfair mom, like most teens do, because she tried to make me mind.

One day, Caleb took a stick and was playing with a snake while he was under the house. When Daddy came home and saw Caleb, he asked him what he was doing. When Caleb told Daddy, he immediately made Caleb get away from it. It turned out to be a venomous coral snake.

My brother Derrick played mostly by himself. Mom said

he was the best child for not getting into things he shouldn't. He was an extremely good child. When Derrick was two years old, he became ill with spinal meningitis. It broke Mom and Daddy's hearts to see him in such bad shape, but Derrick would laugh through it all when Mom and Daddy came to visit him in the hospital. Seeing Derrick laugh the way he did caused Mom and Daddy to be in high spirits with new hope of his recovery.

However, not long after Mom and Daddy came home from their visit, they were notified that Derrick had sadly passed away. Daddy got a permit to carry him back to eastern Tennessee. His funeral was held in Grandpa and Grandma's home.

CHAPTER 7

Aunt Velma married a man named Theodore, and they had four daughters. Connie, Caleb, and I loved being with our cousins we had grown so close to, even though it was only for a short while.

Aunt Velma wanted a son so much that she said she was going to have one even if it killed her. She died while giving birth to her baby son, who also died; she had toxemia.

I wished I had the privilege of growing to know Aunt Velma; I was told she was a very nice Christian woman. I'm glad I was around Uncle Theodore enough to know that he was a kind man, for truly he was.

Uncle Theodore remarried, and he and his second wife had two children. I barely remember them, but I'm sure they would have been fun to be with, the same as our other cousins.

One year, we all loaded up in Daddy's green panel truck and traveled to California. I don't believe sardines had anything on us; we were very tightly packed in the vehicle. However, it didn't take long until Daddy moved his family back to Tennessee. Sometime later, Daddy moved us, along with Grandpa and Grandma, back to California, and once again, Connie, Caleb, and I were with our cousins. On some of our trips, Uncle Rick and his daughter Joy followed along. Sometimes Uncle Brock went with us; other times he hitchhiked.

Daddy moved Mom, Connie, Caleb, and I, along with Grandpa and Grandma, into a two-story upstairs apartment.

I used to dress up in Mom's clothes and jewelry and sit on the bed with Grandma. I sang and would have her repeat the songs. We had lots of fun, laughing and singing.

While Caleb and I were looking out our window and I was holding a pop bottle, a boy came out of his downstairs apartment and started arguing with us. I got mad and threw the bottle on top of his head. He had to have stitches, which caused our daddy to get into a terrible argument with the boy's daddy, almost to the point of fist fighting. Mom was very nervous and hoped Daddy wouldn't go for his gun.

Daddy occasionally took Mom, Connie, Caleb, and I to the beach. To me it was breathtaking and also a joy to see Daddy carrying Mom around, playing with her.

Daddy moved us into a house near a park that had a swimming pool. Mom and Daddy let us play there, except when Daddy was asleep. Caleb and I asked Daddy if we could go there when he was half-asleep. We knew he would say yes.' We thought we would make it home before he awoke.

By the time we remembered to go home, we didn't know if he was awake, so we ran home as fast as we could. When we saw him wide awake and waiting for us, we knew we were in big trouble.

Most of our punishments were standing in the corner, or we had to put our noses in a circle Daddy drew on the wall. Caleb and I would turn and stick our tongues out at each other. Sometimes Daddy whipped us with a belt. I love my daddy, he was precious to me, but until I grew into my middle teens, I just thought of him as my unfair daddy because he tried to make me mind.

One pretty summer day, Caleb and I chased a big female cat into a lady's yard. When she came out of her home, we just knew we were in trouble. Instead, she was very nice and gave us a male kitten, which we took home in hopes we could keep it. Daddy said yes and named it Tiger.

Mom never cared much for animals, but Tiger became a very special member of our family and another traveling companion. Daddy showed me how to make a simple cat house out of a cardboard box. Between Tiger and Tiny Tears, they kept me pretty busy. I was either making things for Tiger to play with in his house or playing with Tiny, except when Caleb and I weren't playing or fighting with each other.

Caleb became ill with the measles and ran an extremely high fever, causing him to hallucinate.

When Mom saw him climb on the headboard of her bed, she asked him what he was doing. He told her he was trying to get away from a giant piece of cheese that was chasing a shoe. Mom knew she had to try her best to doctor him back to health as quickly as possible, and she succeeded.

When it was time for Caleb to start school, it was about as scary as his encounter with the giant cheese for him. Since Mom didn't have a cure for that, he was stuck with school. He was doing fairly well until it started raining very hard, causing him to get more scared than ever. He wanted Mom, so he jumped up from his desk and ran out of his class. He heard someone yell, "Catch him!" which caused him to run even faster. He ran out into the rain and was lost, scared, and crying. The rain eased up, and a nice old man with great compassion saw the little frightened boy and asked him if he knew where he lived. Caleb said no.

The man took Caleb's hand and walked around with him. Finally, Caleb pointed to his home. The man knocked on the door. When Mom answered it, he and Caleb explained what happened. She thanked the man for helping Caleb and then the man left. That's what the Bible calls a Good Samaritan in Luke 10:33: "But a certain Samaritan, as he journeyed, came where he was: and when he saw him, he had compassion on him."

I was a year late in starting school. I was told it was because of my birth month. We never got to stay in one school for very long because of our constant moving. When Connie, Caleb, and I were kids, it was scary to start in new schools. We moved again into a two-story apartment downstairs. One sunny afternoon, Uncle Brock and Caleb were sitting on our steps when they saw a toy truck on the neighbor's step. Uncle Brock told Caleb to play with it. Mom heard Uncle Brock and told him not to teach Caleb to play with things without permission.

We bought our first TV while we lived in Southern California, which I felt was a special treat for us We also had inside bathrooms. Wow, a TV and inside bathrooms! I felt like we were up there with the movie stars!

We moved into another two-story house. No matter where or what kind of home we lived in, Mom always tried her best to keep it as clean and presentable as possible. She also loved flowers and planted them everywhere we lived. Daddy was always a hard worker and a good provider. These were precious memories. Here are more precious ones I hold dear to my heart, like the time when Mom made Tiny Tears clothes for me.

I would go off by myself for hours at a time, playing with Tiny, changing her clothes, and playing with my tea set. Connie was more into board games, and Caleb played with his BB gun and marbles. I liked marbles also.

Daddy hurt his back at work and had to be admitted into the hospital. Connie, Caleb, and I, not knowing anything about insurance, gathered up our toys and sold them to a neighbor lady to pay Daddy's doctor bill. I kept Tiny as I couldn't say goodbye to her. Mom got mad at the lady because she felt we had been taken advantage of, so Mom took us and the money back to the lady and she returned our toys.

When Daddy came home from the hospital, he couldn't go back to work for a while, so we siblings had both parents keeping an eye on us, especially me and Caleb.

Daddy caught us fighting as usual. All of Daddy's other punishments failed, so he gave his new technique a try. He took his belt and made us whip each other. Before we did, we talked it over and agreed not to whip each other hard. Caleb told me to go first, so I whipped him very easy. When it was his turn, he wore me out.

Daddy was peeking around the corner and got tickled, but I didn't see it as being funny. I got over the welts on my rump, and Caleb and I started playing nice together for two days. Then we were at it again.

CHAPTER 8

Once again, Daddy moved us back to Tennessee. We settled into a small two-bedroom house. Daddy took us to visit one of his old friends, as we had done in the past. Daddy's friend was older than Daddy and lived by himself, but he and Daddy were good friends. Connie, Caleb, Joy, and I loved playing in the old man's watermelon patch. He always gave us one when we went to visit. One time the old man started asking Mom and Daddy if I could spend nights with him. At the time, they trusted him enough to let me.

I spotted his snuff on the shelf and wondered how it tasted. As I was putting some in my mouth, I inhaled it and got choked.

On another visit, I spotted his tobacco and tried it. I thought I was doing it right by spitting out the tobacco and swallowing the juice. I got so sick, I thought I was dying. On my third sleepover, though, he told me to get in the bed with him, so nothing would get me in the night. Of course, I was very young and didn't think anything of the request, so I climbed into his bed to get ready to go to sleep. It was this night that he molested me by rubbing his hands on my privates.

The next day, when Mom and Daddy came to get me,

they noticed I was acting differently. They got suspicious and privately asked me if he hurt or touched me on my private body parts. I was scared and said no, but nevertheless, they never let me stay with him again.

When we visited Grandpa and Grandma Crawley, Uncle Jonathan, Caleb, and I occasionally played cowboys. We climbed tall, slim trees and rode them to the ground for our horses.

In one of our episodes, Uncle Jonathan and I talked Caleb into being a horse thief and Caleb agreed. We hung him in a tree in the front yard and then we ran around to the back of the house, shooting our wood guns.

A little later, we remembered that we had left Caleb hanging. We ran to save him. By the time we got to him, he was kicking, trying his best to get his fingers between the rope and his neck to keep from choking to death. Uncle Jonathan and I finally managed to get the rope off and lay him on the ground. He was gasping for air. We came very close to killing him, as he almost choked to death. He survived, but it scared us terribly, and we never tried to use him for a horse thief again. We were afraid to tell our parents, so we kept quiet for a long time.

Uncle Rick and Joy lived nearby. Occasionally, he brought her to Grandma Crawley's to play with us. However, Connie never played with us much. She mostly stayed with the adults.

On one of Joy's visits, Caleb and Uncle Jonathan started chasing us. We got tired and told them to stop. They refused, so Joy and I chased them to the back of the house, where they climbed a tall, slim tree. They thought they were safe until we sawed them down. They landed on saw briers across the road near the creek behind Grandma's house. Joy and I weren't worried about their bones at the time, but I'm glad they weren't broken.

After they brushed themselves off and were no longer mad at us, they helped us catch crawdads. After we were through playing with the crawdads, we turned them back into the creek. I loved watching them swim.

Daddy, Mom, Connie, Caleb, and I lived a half mile from Grandpa and Grandma's. There was a pond in the field behind our home. This pond not only furnished the cows drinking water, but it was a pool for us kids.

Uncle Jonathan, Caleb, and I dragged an old car hood from Grandma's to the pond, turned it upside down, and used it for our boat. We were having a good time paddling around. My dog, which was a stray and whose name I don't recall, joined in and started swimming along beside us. He seemed to be having more fun than I was. I didn't know how to swim, but I sure wanted to learn, so I copied my dog and gave it a try. I succeeded, and that was my first swimming lesson—taught to me by my dog!

At this time, Daddy was making fifty cents per hour building fences across from our home near the woods. He saw a bird's nest and climbed the tree and found two baby hawks. He brought them home and helped Caleb and me raise them. One hawk died.

Daddy would stand in our yard and hold up food, and the remaining hawk would fly down and take it from Daddy's hand. The hawk sat on the pole near the mailbox. To us, it was an amazing sight to watch the hawk. We also enjoyed watching the people as they seemed to be enjoying themselves as they drove by and watched the hawk. Eventually the hawk flew away and never returned. It was for the best, because

Daddy got word that some farmers were threatening to shoot it, which made him mad.

Another time, Connie, Joy, and I, along with our female cousins, tossed our clothes on the bank, except for our underwear, and were playing in the pond. Caleb, Uncle Jonathan, and some other male cousins showed up and took our clothes and hid them. We were angry and embarrassed, but we had no choice but to get out and find them. We never stayed angry long; we just found other things to do.

Uncle Jonathan, Connie, Caleb, and I wondered what it was like to smoke. We tore a paper bag into strips and rolled corn silk in them. We got tickled because they looked like giant cigars. After lighting those up, they caught on fire, but we managed to take a puff of our so-called cigarettes before the fire reached our lips. They tasted terrible and caused us to cough and gag like crazy. It was during one of these small family get-togethers that one of my male relatives took advantage and fondled me. He wasn't much older than me, and I guess he was at the age where boys begin to get curious. He never again tried anything like that, but it was something that I have never forgotten.

Another incident happened later on. My daddy had gotten drunk, as usual, but this time was different. Daddy came in from work and went to bed and called me in to his bedroom. Mom said no to me in a whisper. He called for me again, and that time I went. When I got into the room, he tried to molest me. He didn't get that far, but he tried. The next day, when he came home from work, I jumped behind Mom to hide. It was then that he realized what he had tried to do; he said that it would never happen again—and it didn't. He stayed true to his word. I held on to the upset feelings toward him for a long time. Once I got older, I finally forgave him.

It was around the same time when I was a child that we lived next to a strawberry patch where we picked strawberries for a living. Caleb and I filled our baskets half full of leaves and put berries on top to hide the leaves. When the owner dumped our baskets of berries into his truck, the few berries went into his truck and the leaves flew everywhere. Daddy was embarrassed because even though there were other kids there, Daddy had no doubt which kids would do such a thing. When Daddy called me and Caleb to him, we had to admit we were the guilty ones, and of course we got into trouble again.

Our next job was picking green beans. This time, Cousin Joy helped. She, Caleb, and I stole beans from other workers' sacks to finish filling up ours. We never got caught, which was lucky for Joy because Uncle Rick had a habit of severely punishing her.

There came a time when Joy was still young that Daddy had to come to her rescue. Joy believed that if Daddy hadn't, Uncle Rick would have killed her. Whether good or bad, we definitely never lived dull lives, no matter what!

Mom and Daddy had a hard time trying to keep me from bringing stray dogs and cats home. I even befriended a rat that I fed. It lived in our loft, but I had to say goodbye to it because we moved to the other side of town, and I wasn't allowed to take it with me. We had yet another outhouse. This time there was a cornfield in the back of our small log house.

Connie, Caleb, and I had to ride the bus a little further to school, but I didn't mind. I wasn't in any hurry to get there, except to play the same old-fashioned games at recess that Mom and Aunt Rena played, such as Red Rover and three-legged races. Basketball was Aunt Rena and Connie's favorite. Mom pretty much liked them all. Uncle Jonathan, Caleb, and I liked riding small tree limbs and playing marbles, which was my favorite.

I had to repeat the second grade. I guess I just couldn't keep my mind still long enough to learn much of anything. I also was afraid the other kids would laugh at me for not being as smart as they were.

Daddy and Uncle Rick made moonshine in the cornfield. They were reported to the Feds, who chased them through the cornfield and around to the front of our home, then across the road and through the woods, where Daddy was arrested and put in jail.

Uncle Rick ran out of his shoes while outrunning the Feds through the briers that were in the woods. Uncle Rick made it home with briers still in his feet and his clothes were full of them. Joy and I had to pick them out of his clothes, which seemed to take forever. The next day, Uncle Rick was arrested and put in jail. After he and Daddy went to court, they were put on probation.

Soon afterward, while Daddy, Mom, Connie, Caleb, and I were at a store near our home, Daddy saw the man he claimed turned Uncle Rick and him in. As Daddy approached the man to fight, Connie, Caleb, and I cried as we were yelling for Daddy not to fight. Mom was worried that Daddy would use his gun, so she also was telling him to leave the man alone. Daddy finally left him alone and took us home.

Mom and Daddy always left a living room window open so that our cat, Tiger, could come and go as he pleased. Tiger occasionally brought home rabbits to eat on our back porch, but Daddy took them for Mom to cook rabbit suppers. Of course, Daddy gave Tiger some. Mom was glad Tiger didn't try to bring the rabbits through the window.

A severe thunderstorm came while Tiger was in the woods. He stayed gone for several days. We were getting worried about him when he finally came home, but he had pneumonia. He died on our front porch. Tears flowed as Daddy buried him in the cornfield. We had many cats in our lifetime, but Tiger was the best.

CHAPTER 9

We were on the road again, headed back to Florida with Grandpa and Grandma. Connie, Caleb, and I hated to leave our cousins, to whom we had grown so close. When we got hungry during our travels, Dad would pull over and Mom would fix the adults coffee and all of us sandwiches while Connie, Caleb, and I played in the great outdoors. At night Daddy and Grandpa slept on the ground, even when it was raining a little, to give the rest of us more room in the car.

We moved to different towns in central Florida. Uncle Brock, Aunt Elaina, Aunt Rena, and Uncle Josh did the same. All the men worked wherever they could.

Occasionally, when Daddy saw an old abandoned building, he, Mom, Connie, Caleb, and I would sleep in it. Even though I loved the wildlife, I was a little leery of sleeping with them. It was spooky when I saw spiders and heard Mom nervously asking Daddy about snakes, so it took me a little longer than usual to fall asleep.

Daddy finally moved us into an apartment where there was a train that ran nearby our home. Caleb and I wanted to ride on the inside of the train, but the best we could do was jump on the side of it as it slowly moved down the tracks. It was as much fun to jump off as it was on. Of course, it didn't last but a few days. We were reported to our parents. Even though we got in trouble, it was fun while it lasted. What wasn't fun was me getting pushed into the wrong classroom at school by another girl for meanness and the other kids laughing at me. We later moved, along with Uncle Brock and Aunt Elaina, to north Florida. Uncle Joe and his family moved to a different town in Florida.

Now Daddy wanted to move again. Uncle Brock and Aunt Elaina, with their only child, Joannie, who was in diapers, stayed behind. Grandpa and Grandma also stayed. After we moved south, we found out that Grandpa admitted Grandma into a mental institution.

A while later, moved to a migrant camp in south-central Florida that had seasonal showers, where we got our drinking water. Mom had Connie, Caleb, and me take turns carrying water. I was very tired of carrying it because we had to carry it often while we lived in Tennessee.

One time I decided it wasn't my turn and blurted out that I wasn't going to carry it because it wasn't my turn, but with Mom's higher authority, she made it my turn. I not only had to carry one bucket, but two. I got mad but kept that to myself. It's a wonder she didn't try to knock my head off as it was.

One day, after about a week of riding the school bus, it came to my stop, and as I got up from my seat in the back, I saw and heard a boy say to another boy that he liked my blond hair. When I got off the bus, a jealous girl, Mariam, who was much bigger than me, started beating me up because she liked the boy who had made that statement. The after-school beatings went on for several days. The last day, as Mariam was beating me up, her sister was going to jump in to help her. Connie, being pretty tough, stopped the sister. I don't know why Mariam's sister wanted to help her, as Mariam was winning.

In 1959, we moved a little over ten miles further south to a small town that I instantly fell in love with and called my home. Daddy worked in a packinghouse. We lived in a small community in a one room shack with an inside bathroom. I felt rich once more!

Caleb and I were still fighting with each other. He got mad at me. I don't remember why, but he grabbed a butcher knife to throw at me. I knew I was in trouble. I ran into the bathroom. Just as soon as I shut the door, the knife stuck in it. Not long afterward, while we were in our yard, I picked up a long, slim pole and tried to knock him out with it.

Occasionally, Caleb and I played chicken with knives and darts, throwing them between our fingers and toes, even seeing how close we could get to each other's head.

Caleb tried to throw a dart under my arm, but instead, it stuck in it. When I pulled it out, I started screaming as I ran around our small tar-papered shack that I called castle, acting as though I were dying. I can't imagine how I would have acted if the dart had hit my head. That has always been one of my downfalls—I never really think of the consequence of my actions. I will tell of some very serious ones as I write.

CHAPTER 10

Mom, Connie, Caleb, and I thought our traveling days were over. When Daddy told us we were moving back to east Tennessee, we siblings cried. Daddy said when the packinghouse season started again, he would move us back. We stopped crying, but we didn't know if we would ever see our little town again. When the season began, sure enough, Dad moved us back.

In 1960, we moved to a trailer park near a migrant camp. Every one of my friends and I just called it "the camp." Daddy started working at a dairy company about three blocks from the trailer park (I just call it "the park" most of the time). During this time, we experienced our first hurricane when Hurricane Donna ripped through our area. Connie, Caleb, and I were used to bad storms while living in Tennessee. Since we had never seen the storms throw things around and they had never harmed us, we didn't think this would be any worse, so we siblings weren't very scared. We didn't know how dangerous hurricanes really were. Daddy took Mom, Connie, Caleb, and me to the dairy with some water and food to wait it out. Caleb and I always found something to do, no matter where we were, even if it was just clapping our hands with each other.

Donna calmed down, but Daddy said we were in the eye of the storm. We siblings thought we had seen the last of her. Connie headed toward the door to open it, and Mom and Daddy yelled for her to stop. But it was too late—she opened the door just as Donna blew it wide open with Connie holding on to the knob. Mom and Daddy struggled to save her. Just as soon as they pulled her back inside the building, the door blew off from the bottom hinge.

We watched part of the dairy's walled fence fall apart and debris fly and fall everywhere. Daddy was willing to risk his life to get into the other part of the building where he could get us something to eat and drink if our food and water supplies ran out before Donna was finished.

Uncle Jonathan and Aunt Rena hadn't been living in the area long before Donna came through. They waited Donna out in a packinghouse with their six small children. They didn't know if they would see another day, and neither did we, but we all survived without a scratch. When Donna was finally over, our town and the surrounding areas looked like a war zone.

Not long after, Daddy got the sad news that Grandpa was found dead in a dump site near a canal, possibly from Hurricane Donna.

In the meantime, other kids started picking on me. Daddy said that the next time I came home crying, he was going to whip me. When I started taking up for myself, the bullies backed away. The relief felt so good that I got the big head and became a bully myself. To all I bullied, I am truly sorry!

Connie became best friends and inseparable with a girl named Melinda. Connie helped Melinda with her chores. Connie and Melinda weren't old enough to go to bars;

however, they sneaked into one that was near Russell's pool hall. They stayed close to the back door to listen to the jukebox. They stayed on the lookout for Melinda's stepdad just in case they had to make a quick getaway. While Connie and Melinda were listening to the jukebox, in walked Melinda's stepdad. They saw each other at the same time, and out the door Melinda and Connie ran. They were afraid they wouldn't be allowed to run around with each other anymore, but to their surprise, they were.

In 1962, through Melinda, I met her cousin Lizz. Melinda knew I had a Suzy Smart doll and asked me to show it to Lizz. However, Lizz wasn't a doll person. I had given up Tiny Tears for Suzy Smart, and since Lizz wasn't a doll person, I gave up Suzy Smart for Lizz. I'm glad I did because Lizz was more fun, and we became best friends. Through Lizz, I met a boy name Bo and his two brothers. Bo would turn out to have a huge positive impact on my adult life. These brothers became really good friends to me, Connie, and Caleb. Lizz and the boy were from west-central Alabama. Some of our other friends were Roberto, Tommy, Brentley, and Sam.

CHAPTER 11

In 1963, Uncle Brock moved his family from north Florida and into the trailer park near us. A little later Uncle Sut moved his family into the park. We felt that we were a community in itself.

Because Connie, Caleb, and I were so far behind in school, we had to go to special education classes, as did some of our friends.

It didn't take me, Connie, and Caleb long to find out about a swimming area at the lake at about four miles from our home. Caleb, Lizz, two of our other friends, and I were swimming, and I can't remember who, but I heard someone yell, "There goes an alligator!" When I looked, I saw it go under. Not realizing the danger, we kept on swimming. We walked to the lake as often as we could. We swam all day, then talked and walked all the way home.

After Lizz's parents met mine, we were allowed to spend nights with each other. I thought I would die if I had to spend one day without my friends. Mom liked them also, but I had chores to do. Lizz helped me with mine and I did the same for her, so we could have more time for each other.

To me, our town seemed more like home. I liked our little town, but we never lived there long enough to make close friends. I believe everyone needs close friends to lean on. It's sad on my part because I ruined some of my friendships along life's road that I regret.

South Florida is known for its black dirt (muck). Our town has yearly festivities to spotlight the rich, black dirt for which it is known. Now, back to the school years—everything was such fun; I felt so happy and carefree, except when I had to go to school.

So Caleb and I started skipping school. We would walk to the lake and hide in tall weeds. I thought I was smart enough that I didn't need to learn anything else. I sure didn't understand the true meaning of a good education. I have wished a thousand times in my older years that I would have followed wise advice, toughed it out no matter how hard things got, and stayed in school. The Bible says in Proverbs 8:11, "For wisdom is better than rubies; and all the things that may be desired are not to be compared to it." Occasionally, Lizz and I skipped school alone. Occasionally, another friend skipped with us. We hid in weeds under the long wooden bridge that crossed over to get to the lake.

While Caleb and I were walking alone to the lake instead of going to school, we decided to make a new hideout in tall weeds along the canal bank. Although we'd never seen any gators in that area, there's no telling how many of them were around. On our way to our new hideout, we stopped at a store with money Caleb had and got some things to play with to keep us busy while waiting for school to be let out.

Grandma Crawley and Uncle Jonathan came down to spend time with us. Uncle Jonathan was close to my age, so he skipped school with Caleb and me. We finally talked Connie into skipping, assuring her that we wouldn't get caught, so she went with us to our little hut. Uncle Jonathan and Caleb started fishing in plain view. Connie and I stayed hidden. An officer saw the brave fishermen and stopped to check them out. When the officer didn't believe the fishermen's story, the officer told them he was going to report them to their parents. Caleb yelled, "Come on out, Alice—you were in on it too." Of course, Connie had to come out as well. We were never able to convince her that it would be safe for her to participate in any more of our adventurous activities. We also had to face our parents, who weren't very pleasant.

Caleb and I occasionally played chase. On this particular day, as I was chasing him around our neighbor's small trailer, Caleb told me to stop because he saw broken glass. I refused, so he tried to jump over it, but instead he landed on it. It cut his foot to the point that it was barely hanging on, and it turned white as a sheet instead of bleeding. I'm glad Dad wasn't drunk, so Mom could get him to rush Caleb to the hospital. I'm also thankful Caleb didn't lose his foot. If he had, I would have had a hard time accepting it. My stubbornness has always caused hardships.

After Caleb's foot healed, he, Lizz, and I, along with other friends, sneaked into our friend Todd's dad's pasture to ride his horses. We were having a ball with no worries, when out of the blue a stallion appeared and started chasing us. I believe I had a death hold on my riding partner. If I had gone down, there was no way I was going alone. We held on for dear life and managed to ride the horses to the fence. We escaped without getting seriously hurt.

There were days Lizz and I walked around in the camp in light rain showers with the sun shining. It was very soothing, and we walked, talked, and sang. I never claimed to be a good singer, but nevertheless I enjoyed it. We also went to the theater to watch our favorite icons of the day. While we were watching a movie featuring one of our favorite singers, Lizz and I started screaming just to see if anyone would join in— it worked. It sounded as though everyone were screaming. Connie was embarrassed and mad at me. She was pretty much the quiet one. Caleb, Lizz, and I were different, and we were always thinking of new schemes.

Lizz and I started stealing things some when we were young. We stole a girl's purse, then took her money and threw her purse in tall weeds near her home. We felt bad about it later, because she was a sweet and kind girl. She never bothered anyone.

Caleb, Lizz, two of our friends, and I would go to the swimming pool near our school. It cost a quarter to get in. I stole some dimes from the girls dressing rooms and bought soft drinks from the machine at the pool when we took breaks.

Once, while I was in my dressing room, I left a dime that legally belonged to me. On my swimming break, I went to get it, but it was gone. I was hurt and ready to fight the guilty one. Then it felt like someone slapped my heart and spoke to me, saying, "That's how those others feel when you steal from them." I calmed down. I had never felt anything like that before.

Lizz and I met Roberto's sister, Anne, and us three became best friends and went swimming together, but Anne didn't go with us on this next adventure. Caleb, Lizz, some other friends, and I climbed over the pool's fence after closing hours. We were having a good time until we were reported. When we saw the police coming, we climbed back over the fence and started to run, but before the officers could get out of their car, some of our friends escaped. The officers stopped the rest of us and were putting everyone in the car who fit the description.

The water had darkened my hair, so the officers weren't going to put me in the car because they were looking for a light blond-haired girl. I just stood there soaking wet waiting for them to drive away. Caleb and I had done so much together, he didn't think he should go without me, so he gave out his famous yell once more, saying, "Get in the car, Alice—you were in on it too." The officers put me in the car with the rest of the gang and took us to jail. I don't know which was worse, jail or school.

Speaking of school, now I know our teachers were nice and understanding. I'm sure it took a lot of their understanding to survive us kids. Our teacher took our class camping at a known creek—one weekend for the boys, and one weekend for the girls. Lizz and I sat at the campfire talking, laughing, and just having a good time. After bedtime, we sneaked into the water while everyone was asleep. We weren't as quiet as we thought we were being. The teacher heard us and made us get out of the water, not only because we had no business getting out of our tent, but because it was so dangerous.

After getting back home, I spent the night with Lizz. We sneaked a cigarette from her mom, Sandy. We thought Sandy and Lizz's dad, Walt, were asleep, when we heard Sandy say, "Lizz, when you get through with that cigarette, go to bed," Lizz and I looked at each other in shock, and then Lizz replied in a very calm tone, "Okay."

It was her turn to spend the night with me. Thinking that Daddy was asleep, Caleb wanted us to sneak out of the house to walk on the culverts across the little dirt road by our home.

I wanted to but was afraid of getting caught. Caleb finally convinced me that a whipping wouldn't last long. I should have learned from our past experiences that getting caught was very painful, but I went anyway.

It was fun walking on the culverts at night and singing. We thought we had it made until we heard Daddy call us home. He whipped me and Caleb harder than ever. Lizz's eyes got very big, wondering if she were going to get it also. Of course, she didn't, but she did not spend anymore nights with me for a long time. Caleb and I knew it was in our best interest not to sneak out of our home and to stick with swimming.

On one of Caleb's walks to the lake, he dove in for a swim, which he had done in the past. However, the channel lock, when it was open, made the current become very powerful. This time, it took every ounce of strength he could muster to keep from drowning. It was a hard struggle, but he finally made his way to the bank. He had to rest for quite a while until he was strong enough to walk home.

Near our home was a small airport. Daddy became friends with a pilot named Rome. Daddy took pilot lessons. His pilot license from years past couldn't be found. Rome allowed us siblings to fly in his four-passenger Cessna with them. Connie sat up front with Rome while the rest of us sat in the back. Rome and Daddy took turns flying over a large lake. They flew straight up, then made nosedives and did flips. It was awesome. Lizz and Anne were also allowed to fly with me.

CHAPTER 12

An important part of my current life is a man that most people call K. He and his wife, with their two young children, moved into the trailer park from southern Kentucky and became friends with Mom and Daddy. They started working in a packinghouse, while Daddy stayed at the dairy farm. K's wife started having an affair with a man named Al. Mom knew it but kept it to herself for a long time.

Al had an airboat and invited me and K's wife out for a ride. I was excited since I had never ridden on one before, so I never hesitated to take him up on his offer. I was enjoying the beautiful scenery when Al took me by surprise and started doing donuts. It felt as if we were going to flip. I was holding on for dear life and sure was hoping the gators weren't hungry. Then we got stuck in what I thought were water lilies, but later we were told that they were actually hyacinths. It took Al a long time before he got the boat free. I was glad when we made it back to shore. I was more anxious to get off than I was to get on. That was my first and last airboat ride.

A few days later, Bo told me to sneak out of my home at a certain time at night to meet him. He said that if I didn't, he was going to yell for me to come out. Bo knew that Daddy would get mad at me if he heard Bo and that I would meet him to keep him quiet.

I was hoping Bo wouldn't yell, so I took a chance that he would change his mind. When I didn't come out, sure enough Bo yelled. Daddy was watching TV and didn't hear Bo, which surprised me. The next time I saw Bo, he asked me if I had heard him, and I fussed letting him know how important it was for him not to do anything like that again. He agreed.

Lizz and I started going our separate ways; however, we stayed friends and still did things together occasionally. I met Lindie, Sonya, and Dina, and we became very close friends. All of their parents were very good to me, and I love them dearly!

Lindie and I skipped school and stayed in her house while her mom was at work. We saw the truant officer coming toward her house. About the time Lindie jumped in the bed, he knocked on the door and I let him in. He asked her why she wasn't in school. She replied, "I'm shaking all over." He accepted her answer and then left. She meant to say she was shaking from chills from the flu. I was pretty shaken up too thinking he was going to ask me the same thing, but he didn't. While Lindie and I were talking about it, we burst out laughing because she was shaking from fear of getting in trouble.

We tried talking Connie into skipping with us, but she refused and tried her best to talk me into going to school. Believing she was doing the right thing, she told on me. The truant officer came to Lindie's home and took me to school, as he had done when I skipped at Lizz's home. He warned me if I kept it up, I would get sent to the children's home. Connie felt bad and tried to apologize for telling on me, but I wouldn't accept it. As I look back on that incident now, I'm glad she told on me. If she hadn't, I probably would have ended up in worse trouble at that time, so I'm glad she did the right thing!

A female family member of our neighbors moved down with another woman. They were from up north. They moved into the park. Mom and Daddy became friends with them, and everyone seemed to get along well, but it didn't take long until things changed. Daddy went to their trailer and started drinking with them. A little later, I went over, and Mom came as well. We all were sitting around talking, and then all of a sudden Daddy told Mom to go home. She was afraid to say anything to him while he was drinking, so she quietly left. I stayed until I saw Daddy and the women kissing, then I left. I felt sorry for Mom, even though I didn't show it.

In early 1964, my sister Nea was born. My brother Caleb was getting into trouble for stealing. He stole Uncle Brock's car and was sent to the children's home. After he was released, he spent a night with our friend Todd. I left to spend the night with a girlfriend but decided to go home instead. As I got inside our trailer, I heard Daddy beating on Mom in the bedroom. She was crying and begging him to stop. I knew there was nothing I could do, so I left and went walking around, trying to hold back my tears.

Mom and Daddy were friends with a married couple, Teddy and Meredith. Daddy was drunk and told Mom that he and Teddy had made plans to swap wives. Even though Mom was terrified of Daddy's drinking, she couldn't hold her peace and told Daddy that she was going to Teddy to ask him if his and Daddy's plans were true. Daddy got extremely angry and started slapping Mom. Every time she tried to run out the door, he pushed her away while reaching for his gun. They fought a little longer, but she managed to escape and stayed at her girlfriend's home for a few days.

CHAPTER 13

Toward the middle of 1965, my sister Connie married a man named Robby, and they moved to central Georgia, where Robby is from, later that same year. Around that same time, Daddy and Mom had their last child, Micah.

David, Lizz, Bo, and I went to the high school football game, mostly to be with other friends. Some nights, Lizz and I went alone and crawled under the fence. One night, we talked Anna into sneaking in, assuring her that we wouldn't get caught. Just as soon as we crawled under the fence, our teacher saw us, and he yelled for us to stop. Anne did, but Liz and I crawled back under the fence and took off. The next game, Lizz and I went in legally. As badly as we hated to give up our money, we paid it.

On another trip to the game, Lizz and I wondered how many people we could cause to look up at the sky. We pointed up, saying, "Look, do you see that?" We kept pointing and repeating the phrase until everyone at the game, including the football players, were looking up. We had heard that people fell for that stunt, so we gave it a try (it's odd how curiosity works; it sure has gotten me in trouble through life). Well, people began to realize that it was a prank. I heard someone say in a very angry tone, "I'd like to find the brats who started this." Lizz and I knew it was time to split, so we took off for safety. I don't believe skunks had anything on us; we sure were stinkers.

Bo wanted me to marry him, but I said no. Bo was very good to me, he has always been a gentleman, but I felt I was too young for marriage. I met Jeremy. Daddy, Mom, and we siblings were living in a duplex in the park. My friend Dana lived in the other side.

Dana and I made plans to sneak out after bedtime to meet Jeremy and Patrick, whom we had crushes on, so we fixed our beds as though we were sleeping and sneaked out of our windows. Mom usually came in and pulled the cover off my head. She was always afraid that I would smother. I'm glad for whatever reason she skipped it that night.

CHAPTER 14

My friend Dina and I became closer friends. We ran away from home and hid in her girlfriend's home in the camp. On the second day, we saw my mom coming. I didn't want to hide anymore, so I opened the door when she knocked. Mom grabbed my wrist tightly and took me home. A few days later, my girlfriend Carolyn told me she told Mom where I was for my own good. She didn't want to see me get into trouble. She also loved Mom and knew Mom was worried about me. I couldn't stay mad at her, and we remained friends. After some time passed, I thought my friendship with Dina was over because she stopped coming around. Then I was told she had been sent to the children's home.

While I was at home doing my chores, my friend Lida came and asked me if I would run away from home with her. I never had any reason to run away, because Mom and Daddy were good to us as far as providing for us. Plus, after I ran away with Dina, I had no desire to run again, so I said no. Lida said she asked others, but they refused, so I agreed to go. I knew I hurt Mom and Daddy the first time, but I never realized how scared and hurt they really were. I was only thinking of my friend's feelings and my own selfishness.

Lida made plans with some guys she knew to meet us at

the lake to take us out of the state. On the way to the lake, we stopped at a clothing store and stole some two-piece bathing suits. After getting to the lake, we hid in tall weeds along the bank. After waiting on the guys for a while, we became restless and rented a paddleboat from the lake. We paddled our way out into the middle of the small swimming area. This was on a school day. How dumb were we to do such a thing in plain view during school hours?? Nevertheless, we didn't worry about getting caught until we saw the truant officer crossing the bridge headed our way. We knew he had to be looking for us.

We knew our fun was over, but we still tried to get away. We panicked to the point that we couldn't paddle the boat in the direction we wanted to go. We just kept going around in circles. I had learned more about gators' nature by then, but I finally told Linda to jump out and swim. That's when she told me she didn't know how to swim. I thought if a gator were below, it would have to scoot over because I was jumping in. Why in the world I was more afraid of the truant officer than the gator I'll never know, but anyway I swam while pushing Lida and the boat to shore. We jumped out and hid under the bridge, hoping the truant officer couldn't find us, but he did and took us to jail in our stolen bathing suits. I'm glad no one found out they were stolen. We were in enough trouble as it was.

Our parents brought our clothes to the jail. Lida and I were taken to the children's home, where we stayed upstairs in lockup for a month before going to court. After court, the judge sent Lida to her home. He sent me back to the children's home because I had been in more trouble than Lida. Also, I refused to follow the truant officer's warning to stay in school and behave myself.

I felt Lida and I had good times together and were becoming best friends, but since I stayed in the children's home, I didn't know if she or any of my other friends would forsake me. I was placed back upstairs in lockup. My hair was cut very short, which was the standard rule. All the girls in lockup had to scrub their bathroom floor with a toothbrush. Boys were placed in the home, but they were separated by a good distance.

I was watching the girls walk for their exercise when I saw Dina and yelled her name. She looked up at me, and it seemed to me she started crying as she ran inside the building. When I was placed downstairs in the dorm, Dina and I were together again. She was kind-hearted but I was hard-hearted, maybe because of the abuse I had to deal with. We went to church. Part of me didn't mind because it had such a peaceful atmosphere, and I felt good being there.

We also had to go to school, the very place I tried so hard to stay away from, but there was no hiding place, so I was stuck. While I was in class, a boy and I started flirting. We passed notes; one was to excuse ourselves from class to sneak a kiss. We made it outside of the building, but we were caught before our lips connected. Oh well, we can't win them all! We were placed in lockup for our crime of passion.

When we got our privileges back, we returned to the weekly dance, standing at arm's length, which was another standard rule. We didn't mind too much; it was better than nothing. I enjoyed our street dances the most. Even though we had supervision, we all took turns dancing in the form of a privacy fence. In other words, we danced close to each other to block the supervisor's view in order to surround the couple in the middle, so they could sneak a kiss.

Because we didn't get caught, we tried another stunt—playing chicken. The girls stood side-by-side in the field opposite from the boys to see which couple was brave enough to meet in the middle of the field for a kiss. We all walked at the same time, but halfway there, the couples chickened out except me and my sweetie. We accomplished our goal, but just as we were caught. It happened so fast; it was all in that moment. We didn't get into serious trouble—for some reason my guardian liked me.

My friend Nancy and I made plans to run away. We talked it over to include my friend May from my hometown. The next day, somebody told on us, and we were punished. After our privileges were given back, we got to ride on a small cabin cruiser at the beach. Girls and boys were not allowed to be taken together, of course. There were some handsome boys on the beach, but the best we could do was look from a distance. After our boat ride, we were allowed to stay on the beach for a little while.

We were having a good time until one of our girls got caught talking to a boy. Our guardian didn't waste any time taking us back to the home. We were angry with the girl for messing up our fun, and we never had the privilege to go back to the beach.

The home wasn't a bad place. Considering my attitude, I had good times there, and we were never mistreated. I missed Mom and Daddy more than ever, and I got my act together. Even though I only had to stay for a short time, it felt like an eternity, and I could hardly wait to get home. When I was released, I wondered if I still had my friends. I was relieved when they treated me as though nothing had happened and our friendship remained strong.

I had to repeat the seventh grade. I was finally beginning to like school and was trying to do better, but I still had a bad attitude. While I was in school, a new girl was placed in my class. She looked familiar, and I kept thinking, *Where have I seen her before?* Then like a shockwave going through me, I remembered, *That's Mary from Pahokee who used to beat me up.* I kept quiet until after school. Lizz, Anne, and I followed her until we were almost off the school grounds. I stopped Mary and asked if she remembered me, and she said no. I reminded her of the times she used to beat me up and asked her if she would like to try that again. She refused, so I went my way and she went hers.

A few days later, a girl in my class asked me my age. When I told her, she and other classmates laughed at me for being too old to be in their class. It was a month before my sixteenth birthday, so I just quiet.

CHAPTER 15

Bo was still a good friend to me. Even though we had a few harsh words between us, we still hung around together.

While Anne and I were walking in the camp, Bo drove up in his 1955 Mercury. He drove us around on his hood as he had done before. Shortly afterward, he and Anne started dating, and I dated Melinda's brother Samuel.

One day, as Bo was driving all of us around in the camp, Anne asked him if he would teach her and me how to drive and he agreed. When Bo stopped the car to change drivers, Lida walked over to talk to us, and we all went riding. I watched Anne's driving as Lida, Sam, and I sat in the back. Anne's driving looked easy. She drove just fine.

Then it was my turn, and I could hardly wait to get behind the wheel. When the time came, Samuel sat in front to help me. I was doing fine until I got a little too close to the edge of the road. Lida knew it was my first driving lesson, so I scared her, and she screamed, "You're running off the road!" I panicked and instead of pressing the brake, I pressed the gas pedal to the floor. Samuel grabbed the wheel, and we ran into an elderly lady's home and knocked her concrete steps loose, jammed her door, came so close to her gas tank, and broke her gas line from her tank that she used for cooking and heating.

Gas was spewing out like crazy. It's a thousand wonders some of us weren't smoking.

Bo told us to hide before the law got there. I wanted to take the blame, but he insisted that I hide, so I hid with the others. When the law arrived, they had to pry the lady's door open to help her and her dogs outside. I never thought of how hurt or shook up she may have been at the time, but I was glad everything turned out alright with her.

Anne and Bo broke up, and so did Sam and I. Bo moved to Ohio with his new girlfriend and her family. Occasionally, Lizz, Anne, Lida, and I still went for our walks and met guys. Anne met Stan, and he introduced me to his cousin Stanley. For me, it was love at first sight. I felt like he was the very core of my heart. I felt we four were quite a team. It didn't matter to me where we went as long as I was with Stanley. Then, for some unknown reason, Stanley disappeared. I was heartbroken, believing it was over for us.

CHAPTER 16

My friend Sonya and I ran around more together and became best friends. We worked in a packinghouse together.

My daddy's rule was that if I quit school, I would have to get a job and help pay bills. I'm glad he taught me some responsibility. Of course, I didn't feel that way at first, but then I didn't mind because it was just so much fun working with Sonya. Sonya and I laughed, talked, sang, and clowned around. Time flew by and before we knew it, our long working hours were over.

Mom had been working in a different packinghouse with K and his wife, not far from the one where Sonya and I worked. Then K's wife changed packinghouses, and K started bringing lunch to Mom and they ate and talked.

Daddy's mistreatment of Mom and K's wife's mistreatment of him brought Mom and K closer together, and they fell in love. They decided to move to Kentucky. Mom told me I could go with her if I wanted to. I was very tired of moving, and I finally had best friends, so I chose to stay with Daddy. Mom and K moved, and Daddy kept my sister Nae and brother Micah.

One day, I went to Sonya's home and helped her with her chores. When we finished, I started reminiscing about the time when I was still in school. It was on a weekend when I pulled prank phone calls at random from the phonebook. It was just something new to try.

When I returned to school, my teacher was staring at me while he was telling the class about receiving a prank call. I felt like crawling under my desk. He never said who he thought it was, but the way he was staring at me, I knew he knew. Sonya and I decided to give it a try. At least I knew I wouldn't have to face another teacher. Once more, I had no idea who I'd asked if their refrigerator was running and told they'd better catch it. Well, at least it was a clean joke. I had slowed down with my bad language, so the clean joke was a good thing.

Sonya and I accumulated a nice collection of records. We were always learning new dances, when we weren't out doing things—like the time we went with two friends, Willy and Ray, to play chicken at night in a canal. Sonya sat on Willy's shoulder and I sat on Ray's to see who could pull the other off first. It was a blast, but the guys said we had to get out of the water, knowing that gators would show up. When they dropped us off at Sonya's home, she and I couldn't sleep, so we lay there for hours talking until we finally drifted off.

CHAPTER 17

Sonya, Anne, Lida, Lizz, and I loved to walk. We sure got our share of exercise; I believe we got enough for the entire camp. On one of my walks with Sonya, I met Raymond, who was very handsome.

Sonya and I had been going to the skating rink in southern Florida, about sixteen miles from my hometown. We bummed rides as often as we could. Raymond loved to skate, so it wasn't a problem for him to take us.

One particular night, Sonya and I didn't go skating. Instead, she wanted to see her boyfriend, and she didn't want to walk, so we stole her stepdad, Donald's, car. She didn't know how to drive very well, but she got us there in one piece. When we got back to her home, we thought we had the car parked in its proper place. That morning, Donald noticed his car had been moved and asked Sonya about it. She told the truth, and though we didn't get in trouble, we never stole his car again.

Sonya and her boyfriend broke up, and then we met two guys that Daddy's friend Ted introduced us to. Sonya and I nicknamed them Smiley and Happy because they were always jolly.

They took us riding around. We ended up in the town where the skating rink was. It was winter, and we stopped at a bar. Smiley went in and brought us back some daiquiris. We all sat in the car drinking, and it sure tasted good. I finished my third one and had to go to the bathroom. The guys told me to be careful because I had drunk too many. They didn't tell me what a daiquiri was. They must have thought I knew.

Anyway, I told them not to worry, I didn't feel a thing. When I got out into the fresh air, I hit the ground drunk as a skunk, as the old saying goes. I must have looked so funny they couldn't help but laugh at me. Sonya had to help me to the bathroom. She was still laughing, causing me to get tickled and laugh too.

Raymond and I started dating. He took me and Sonya skating more often. He was a good skater; Sonya and I were terrible, but we had a ball trying. As I was holding on to the bar, this young boy grabbed my hand and flew around the rink with me. I'm sure it was obvious to him that I couldn't skate, but I told him anyway and asked him to let go of me. He did. I couldn't stop, so I ran into the bar and almost flipped. If funniest home videos were aired back then, I probably could have won $10,000 just from the expression on my face alone.

While we were at the skating rink, a girl that didn't like Sonya told me she wanted to fight her. I knew Sonya was tough, so I said, "She will fight you after closing time." The girl said okay. I was having too much fun to go outside just for a fight! Closing time came, and when the girl saw me telling Sonya about the fight, the girl left. Sonya got mad at me for making those plans without her knowledge. Then we laughed, and Raymond took us home.

Daddy, Caleb, and I had moved into the camp earlier. Sonya would come over, and we would practice our dancing. Bo broke up with his girlfriend and moved back to my hometown. One day while he was walking by my home, he saw me and Sonya dancing, so he watched for a little while.

CHAPTER 18

Caleb and Sam were still running around together, getting into trouble. One night, Caleb went without him and sneaked out of our home after bedtime. He stole Daddy's car to go joyriding. He was acting suspicious and was chased by the law. Caleb outran them to the house and hid under Daddy's bed. It woke Daddy up, but he kept quiet.

When Daddy heard a knock on the door, he answered it, and there stood an officer. He asked Daddy if he let anyone drive his car, and Daddy said no. The officer told Daddy to go outside and feel his car hood, because it was hot from being driven. Dad felt his hood, and, not knowing how to handle the conversation, he just said, "Well, I'll be, it is, isn't it?" Then they went back inside the house.

When the officer stood in my bedroom door shining his light in my face, he asked me if I drove Daddy's car. I said, "No, I don't know how to drive." After the officer shined his light through the house and found no one else, he left. Daddy told Caleb he could come out from under the bed, and Caleb did.

Another night, Caleb went walking. When the officers saw him, they chased him, and again Caleb outran them. This time, Caleb climbed up a small, slim tree that was in our backyard. The officers shined their lights all around and in the tree. Caleb was slim himself, so he blended in with the branches. The officers gave up and left.

Daddy bought Caleb a plane ticket under Uncle Jonathan's name and sent him to Grandma Crawley's home, hoping to keep him out of town and out of trouble. It didn't work—Caleb came right back and got into more trouble. The judge sent him to different correctional facilities, but Caleb would escape and get caught. One of his worst experiences was going to a reform school located on the other side of a large lake from our hometown at the age of sixteen and seventeen.

Around this same time, Mom came down from Jellico. I was happy to see her and thought that she and Daddy had worked things out and were getting back together. But she got Nae and Micah and went to the bus station to head back to Kentucky. Ray, who was Connie's husband at the time, told Daddy where Mom was. Daddy jumped in his car and tried to stop the bus, but he couldn't, so he came home. Daddy was mad and wanted to know who took Mom to the station. Ray was afraid to tell Daddy at first, but Ray decided to tell confess. Daddy got mad at him for a little while but got over it and they became friends again.

CHAPTER 19

Anne and I were walking in the light rain. The sun was shining, which caused the rain to glitter. I was taking it all in when Bo's brother Wesley walked up to me and offered me five dollars if I would try to get Connie to meet him. I went home and asked her if she would, but she refused. When I told Wesley, he went on his sad way, and I spent my five dollars, although I would have done it for nothing.

On another clear, sunny day, as Sonya and I were walking, she said she met a man named Landon, and he was tall, handsome, twenty-one years old, and separated from his wife. When I met him, I thought that my ex-boyfriends Stanly and Raymond were just as handsome as Landon; however, Stanley was always number one!

When Landon wanted to date Sonya, she told him he would have to get a divorce first. She said he did, and they started dating. I introduced him to Raymond, and we four started double dating. We went skating quite often. Landon's skating was as bad as mine and Sonya's. Landon's friend Greg came down from Upstate New York, to visit him. Since Landon and Sonya weren't serious about each other, they broke up, and she and Greg dated.

Anne and I were walking in the camp. We girls walked

different places, but the camp was our favorite and was convenient. Anyway, Landon and his friends pulled up in a car, and Landon asked me out. I turned him down. This went on for several days. He told me he was divorced. He showed me his divorce papers, in case I didn't believe him; I still refused him. My feelings for Raymond were growing, and I didn't want us to break up.

During another trip to the rink, Sonya, Raymond, and I were having a good time. Sonya and I mastered the art of skating, or at least we got around the rink a few times before falling. We even learned how to skate backward, if one could call it that. I was disappointed because Raymond had to leave before closing time. Landon showed up in his car and came inside. He knew Sonya and I weren't ready to leave, but I was going to anyway. He told Raymond that he would take me and Sonya home and for Raymond not to worry, that he would take care of us. Raymond didn't trust Landon much, but Landon had such a smooth, convincing way about him, it was unreal, so Raymond agreed for Landon to take us home and then Raymond left.

Closing time came and we were on our way home. I was a bit angry, but I loved being with Sonya so much, I kept my anger to myself and went along with them. A few days later, when Landon saw Raymond, he told him we were dating. Raymond came and asked me if it was true, and I told him it was a lie. Nevertheless, Raymond broke up with me and was going to fight Landon. Someone must have warned Landon because he steered clear of Raymond. Raymond was a tough guy. Most of my friends were tough.

Raymond disappeared and went on with his life, so I started dating Landon. He told me he deliberately broke me and Raymond up because he wanted to be with me. I got upset, but Raymond was gone, so I didn't say anything about it. Now that I think about it, I believe Landon, Greg, and Sonya knew Raymond had to leave early from the rink that night, and they had it planned for me and Landon to be together.

After Landon and I dated a little longer, he tried to talk me into giving in to him, but I refused. Unbeknownst to me, Landon had bet Greg that I would give in. One night while Sonya and I were alone, she started trying to persuade me to give in to Landon.

A few dates later, the four of us were on our usual dating routine. Sonya tried to persuade me again to give in to Landon, and this time I did. Then Landon told Greg to pay up. Landon killed two birds with one stone—he got what he wanted from me plus he got paid by Greg. I believe Landon persuaded Sonya into trying to talk me into giving in to him, and that's how I was talked into having sex with Landon. Sonya and Greg got mad at Landon and fussed at him for the way they were tricked, but Landon just laughed, and Greg paid. It broke my heart, but the damage was done—plus it turned out that I got pregnant that night.

Sonya once told me I was too gullible. Now, as I think back, she was too, but maybe not as much as me! I believe if she had known the torment Landon would put me through in the future, she wouldn't have gone along with the schemes. I didn't hold it against her though; I could have said no. We remained friends.

I tried to hide my pregnancy from Daddy as long as I could, but a lady friend of Daddy's told him I was probably going to have a baby. Daddy asked me about it. I said I was.

Without my knowledge, Daddy threatened to have Landon put in jail if he didn't marry me. I called Mom and told her about my pregnancy. She said I could come to Kentucky and she would help take care of me. I didn't love Landon and told him I was going to Mom's. He begged me to stay and marry him, telling me that he loved me. He said that ever since we got together, I was the only girl for him, and he wanted to help me take care of our baby.

After all Landon said and by the way Daddy was talking to me, I believed he was involved and trying to make us get married. And if I didn't go to Mom's, then he would make me and Landon get married. I knew I could go to Mom's, but Landon was my baby's father, so I chose to believe Landon. I told him I would marry him. When Daddy started talking to me about marriage again, I told him Landon and I were getting married.

Out of the blue, Stanly came to see me. It was all I could do to hold back my tears of joy. I didn't know then if I would marry Landon. Stanly found out that I was getting married and asked me not to. My emotions were so mixed up. I was ashamed to tell him that I was going to have a baby and Daddy was making us get married, so I never told him about it. I was ashamed to tell Stanly the whole situation. Stanly said he would be back, and then he kissed me and left. I didn't believe him because he had left me before and stayed gone for a long time. I didn't know when or if I would see him again, so a few weeks later, I married Landon in the spring of 1967, and that's when my hell on earth began.

CHAPTER 20

Landon and I eventually moved to Michigan and lived with his dad, Lou, his stepmom, Joni, and their three children—John, eight years old; Suzanne, six years old; and Rodney, four years old. I had to wash the entire household's clothes on a wringer washing machine. When it broke down, I had to wash on a washboard and wring the clothes out by hand, then hang them on the line. There were heavy blue jeans among all their clothes. I'd seen Mom wash the same way, and her knuckles bled!

My feelings for Landon started growing—but then he told me that the only reason he married me was because Daddy threatened to have him put in jail. I was crushed, not only because of my feelings for him, but because I didn't think Daddy would go that far. Landon saw other women from the beginning. He started going out with Joni's babysitter, Marybelle. Landon was so cold-hearted that he made plans with Joni's brother, Wesley, to listen in on our private time. That morning I overheard them laughing and talking about it. I felt like crawling under a rock.

Anne and Stan married before I did, and she had a baby boy. She and Stan moved to Michigan, not far from me. I was very excited to see her. She also was having marital problems, so we wanted to go back home. Landon gave me the bus fare and Anne had hers. After getting home, I called Landon and told him if he wasn't there when our baby was born, I was getting a divorce. So he moved down. I didn't know if we would get back together, but I felt that he needed to be at our child's birth. We did, however, end up reconciling our relationship.

Landon and I took a trip to Kentucky to visit Mom and K. We all went shopping. On the way back to their home, a nearby train was coming down the tracks pretty fast. K said, "Watch me outrun that train." Mom and I begged him not to try, but he was confident that he could make it. We got a few feet from the train, and just as we were about to cross the track, the train caught up with us. K knew he couldn't make it, so he swerved and drove into a ditch, which kept us from hitting a switchboard. It scared Mom and me so much we got sick to our stomachs. That's the first time I'd ever seen K and Landon turn white as a ghost, especially Landon. I was eight months pregnant.

The next day, Landon and I went back to southern Florida. One night, while Landon and I were riding around, some guys in a car started chasing us, trying to run us off the road. Landon tried to lose them but couldn't. I was afraid we were going to flip, or the guys were going to run us into the deep canal. I told Landon to drive to the police station. When he did, the guys left. Come to find out, Landon was messing with the guys' women, and the guys were out for revenge.

CHAPTER 21

In the middle of 1967, Connie gave birth to her only son, Sean. Landon and I moved in with our friend George and his wife.

Later that year, I was supposed to go out for a ride with Landon, but I changed my mind because I felt very tired. Landon left and was paying more attention to his radio than his driving. He ran off the road and into the wet grass, causing his car to flip upside down in a narrow canal. He had to crawl out of his window and dig his way up the bank. We didn't live far from the scene of his accident, so he walked home and woke me up to get him a change of clothes. He was muddy from head to toe. After he changed clothes, he walked back to the scene to wait for the police. It was a double blessing I had stayed home that morning, because I believe that my baby and I would have been killed.

I was very stubborn, and due to my stupidity, I went to a doctor only once during my entire pregnancy. I developed toxemia so bad my eyes were almost swollen shut. I was so full of poison from the toxemia that an orange color could be seen through my skin. I could feel it sloshing when I moved. I knew it was important to have checkups, but I didn't realize how dangerous the consequences of neglecting them really were.

Soon after Landon's accident, I went into labor. Landon took me to the hospital, and I sat in a wheelchair while I waited for a bed and filled out the paperwork concerning my family history.

Suddenly, the poison came gushing out. It felt very cold. A nurse's aide put me on a bed. More poison came gushing out. By then, I was going into a state of confusion. Then I saw and heard someone, probably the aide, running and yelling, "Get a doctor quick—the baby's already dead!" It scared me into tears. Landon got very angry at the lady who yelled out that terrifying statement. The doctor came rushing in to try to save my baby. Soon he got everything under control and our beautiful daughter was born a little after four o'clock that morning, just a while before Christmas, at the hospital not too far from our home in Florida. I named her Brianna, and we decided to call her Brie for short, after Uncle Sut's youngest daughter.

During the first two months of her life, she cried more than a typical newborn baby should. Other young parents told me that she had colic and that it would go away.

K and Mom came down from Kentucky and stayed at Uncle Brock and Aunt Elaina's. While I was visiting them, Brianna started crying extremely hard again. When I told Mom that Brie had been crying like that for a long time, Mom told me that I needed to take her to the emergency room and that she would go with me. Landon took us to the local hospital that night.

The doctor diagnosed Brianna with meningitis. She was kept in isolation in an incubator for a few weeks. We had to wear masks and couldn't even get near her. She was so tiny and looked so helpless and pitiful—all I could think about was the fact that I couldn't help her. I was told through the grapevine that other babies had died at that time from that disease.

My mind was so wrapped up in Brianna's situation that I didn't try to find out if it was true. Fortunately, Brianna was discharged from the hospital just in time for us to celebrate the holidays! I was so happy, I couldn't have asked for a better gift. Brianna is a walking miracle in more ways than one, and I praise the Lord for sparing her life again. I have yet to lose a child. My heart goes out to those who have!

Even into today, I have always felt guilty, wondering if neglecting my pregnancy checkups contributed to my baby's meningitis. To have lost her would have been devastating. The concern Landon showed toward me while I was in labor, then toward Brianna when she had meningitis, led me to believe he truly loved us, and it encouraged me to hold on to our marriage. I also felt it was vitally important for my daughter to be raised by both parents.

While Mom and K were staying at Uncle Brock's, Daddy came bursting through the door and pointed his gun at K. However, something changed his mind about shooting him and left. The next day, Landon and I were visiting Mom and K. Mom and I were in Uncle Brock's bedroom, and I was changing Brianna's diaper; Daddy stopped by again and called for me, but Landon went to the door and told Daddy in a hateful manner that I was busy. Daddy stormed in and started fighting with Landon. They fought their way into the bedroom and started falling toward the bed where Brianna was laying. I rushed to grab her out of the way just as they fell on the spot where she had been seconds before. Daddy and Landon fought their way back into the living room and landed on the recliner. Landon managed to get Daddy in a headlock, and then they calmed down and Daddy left. Mom and K went back to Kentucky not long afterward.

CHAPTER 22

My marriage to Landon was going from bad to worse. He was constantly telling me Brianna wasn't his. At that point I had already grown so very weary of his accusations. It had been raining hard, but it finally slowed down to a light sprinkle. I wrapped Brie in her blanket and headed for the door. Landon asked me where I was going, so I told him that I was taking her to her real daddy. He said I wasn't taking her anywhere. After more arguing, I left with Brianna and Landon went to his dad's, who had recently moved back from Michigan. Shortly after I returned home, Landon arrived and the arguing continued. He said he was going to move in with his dad, so I threw his clothes outside, where they landed in a mud puddle. He picked them up and pitched them back inside of our small one-bedroom mobile home, where I would then pick them up and throw them back outside. After a few more pitching back and forth, he took his clothes and left.

My old friend Sam and I had always been close. He knew I loved to listen to my vinyl records, so he brought me some. One of the songs was "Your Good Girl's a Gonna Go Bad." I never cheated on Landon, at least not until this point. Sam and I started kissing, and then it went on from there. I wasn't out for revenge, it just felt good to believe that I was important to somebody. This continued for several days. I finally told Sam that we had to stop. He understood and was sweet about it, and we kept it a secret and left it alone. Landon and I reconciled.

CHAPTER 23

In the beginning of 1968, Bo married a girl named Dana, and they moved to the north-central part of Alabama. Around that same time, K brought Mom down from Kentucky again, so she could go to court and finalize her divorce from Daddy. The following day, once the divorce was final, Mom and K got married. Connie and I attended the ceremony. Uncle Brock was K's best man. K's sister-in-law was Mom's maid of honor. After Mom and K's marriage, they went back to Kentucky, and a few months later, Mom and K's son, my half-brother, Kyle Anthony, was born.

Landon and I had moved to a town nearly directly in the center of Tennessee and lived with Landon's mom, Marie, and stepdad, Tim. After continued fighting, Landon left me and Brianna there and moved back to Florida. Tim paid my bus fare back to Florida while he and Marie kept Brianna for a little while. After I got home, Landon and I reconciled once again. Marie and Tim soon moved back to Florida also. Marie started working in a small country store soon after they were settled.

Landon and I separated… again.

Brianna was eighteen months old when Landon stopped denying her as his child, but his next uncalled-for remark was worse. He told me if I took Brianna out of the state, he would kill me. Leaving the state had never crossed my mind. When he said that, I got mad, and since Connie and her husband, Ray, were moving back to Georgia, I asked Connie if I could come. She said yes. After staying for a couple of weeks, Ray paid my bus fare back home, and I went to live with Daddy. I went to the country store and asked Marie if she knew where Landon was. She said no. I didn't believe her and told her to tell Landon I was back. Then I went back to Daddy's. I felt if he was going to kill me, now was his chance.

One night soon after, while I was watching TV, Landon came in uninvited, took Brianna out of her playpen, then said, "Now you're going to find out how it feels," and then he stormed out the door. An hour or two later, he brought her back to me. He just came in, put her back in her playpen, and left without saying a word. I thought, *Well, he must not have been able find a babysitter so he could go out with his lady friend.*

Once again, Landon and I reconciled and moved in with Marie and Tim not too far from where we had once been. I liked them, but it hurt me when they took up for Landon's wrongdoings. Maybe I was getting paid back for mine, for the Bible says in Galatians 6:7, "Be not deceived; God is not mocked: for whatsoever a man soweth, that shall he also reap." I never realized I had sown so much!

Living with my in-laws was hard at times. For example, when Tim and I were going home from seeing Marie at the store, he blurted out, "If you don't prove to me that you're a good mother, I will take Brianna away from you." I didn't understand why he said that, unless it was his beer talking.

On another day, he began to speak vulgar to me. I kept silent until he did it again, and then I felt I needed to tell

Landon. Landon got mad at me and told Marie. When she asked me about it and I said it was true, she got mad at me and called me a liar.

Sometimes they all made me feel trapped, as though I was in prison, except for Landon's brothers, Billy Joe, Danny, and Neil.

One evening, a thunderstorm was headed toward us. I felt tired and laid down on my bed with Brianna since I didn't have her playpen to put her in. After Brianna went to sleep, I drifted off listening to the rain outside. But when I woke up, my baby was gone. I searched the house, calling for her, but she wasn't there. Panic set in. I started crying as I ran out into the rain, yelling for her. It was raining so hard, I could hardly see my hand in front of me. A friend of mine heard me and came to help me find Brianna. She helped me search everywhere, but still nothing. She told me to calm down and to call the law.

The rain slowed down to a sprinkle, and up the driveway came Tim and Marie with Brianna. Tim saw that I was about out of my mind with worry, so he tried to make me feel guilty by telling me he took Brianna because I fell asleep while leaving her awake and that he was just teaching me a lesson. Marie fussed at him for telling me that lie. I was so relieved to see Brianna safe that I let his stinging remark go. I was so heartbroken and lonely that I desperately wanted to see my brother Caleb, but he was incarcerated.

CHAPTER 24

By the end of 1969, Mom and K's second child, my half-sister, Kay, was born. Not too long after, K visited his sister in Ohio and went to church with her and got saved. He came back home, and he and Mom went to church and she got saved too. Mom said that while she was at the altar, the Lord showed her a pack of cigarettes leaving her body and three drops of blood dripping down from heaven. Mom believes the three drops of blood represented God the Father, his Son Jesus, and the Holy Ghost. The departure of the cigarettes represented the Lord taking the craving from Mom because she didn't have the willpower to stop smoking on her own. Ever since that night she has never craved them anymore.

Soon afterward, K's sister Margarete went to church with them and gave her heart to the Lord and got saved also. I believe the Lord spared Mom and K's lives because they, along with Margarete, became a singing group. After Mom and K's last child, Dale, was born and became a man, he and his friend joined the group also. Another young man that they knew occasionally helped them by playing the drums.

CHAPTER 25

By this time, Landon and I had separated again, and he was seeing a new girl named Rachael who moved to town. She looked so much like me that people who saw us from a distance couldn't tell us apart.

Landon said Rachael was jealous of me and was going to fight and beat me. He told her that could go both ways. However, when I went to her house and asked her about her remark, she denied it. Whether or not she actually said it, I believe Landon really just wanted two women to fight over him.

Even though she was seeing Landon, she had a boyfriend named Mel. I knew him when I was in my teens. He was very handsome, and I liked him back then, but not sexually. I kept my feelings to myself about Mel. While Landon and Rachael were having their affair, Mel asked me out and I went. When she found out, she asked me about the affair between Mel and I, and I told her that we had gone all the way. We had a few words and then she left. This time I killed two birds with one stone: I got revenge on Landon, and I got to go out with Mel. I believe Mel was out for the same reasons. I had prepared to fight with Landon if he found out, but he never did, which surprised me. Anyway, Landon stopped seeing her as far as I knew.

Landon became a long-distance truck driver. He left me living with his parents for most of our marriage. We never had a home of our own. He was still his cruel self. He made plans for one of his fellow truckers to adopt Brianna, and the man's wife was all for it also. They fell in love with Brianna during some of our visits to their home. I had no idea what was going on until Landon dropped that bomb on me. I told Landon there was no way I was giving up my baby, and he never mentioned it again. Why Landon wanted to hurt me throughout our entire marriage was beyond me. Maybe it was because Dad made him marry me, and that was his revenge. But he could have freed himself at any time. As a matter a fact, I tried to get him to divorce me and let me pull my life back together. He said I was his wife and he could do anything he wanted to me.

Landon, Brianna, and I moved in with Lou and his family in the camp. While Landon and I were on the porch, his friend Michael came to visit. Michael sat in one of our chairs, and suddenly Landon pushed me in Michael's lap and told us to go have fun. I was deeply embarrassed and hurt. Although Michael knew Landon's cold heart, he was still shocked at what had just happened. Later, Landon brushed it off as a joke. Women would drive by Lou's home and yell for Landon to come out to be with them.

Landon finally moved us out on our own. I had been feeling ill for a long time. I would lay down after putting Brianna in her playpen. Even though she was old enough to not be in a playpen, it was my babysitter. I sure didn't want to go to sleep while she was awake. I was drifting off to sleep when Landon invited his friend Jason and Jason's girlfriend, Enid, over to play cards. Landon wanted me to be his partner. I said no, I didn't feel good, but he kept on until I got up. We played a few rounds, and then Jason saw Enid and Landon playing with each other's feet and legs under the table. Jason jumped up and punched Landon in the face, giving him a black eye, and told him to leave his girlfriend alone. Then he stormed out with her in tow. Landon had to be out of his mind to try such a thing, knowing Jason's tough reputation. I felt that Jason and I were set up so Landon and Enid could be together as much as possible.

People put up with abuse for different reasons. Part of me believes that my reason was for Brianna's sake. I know the other part was because I still loved Landon, and occasionally he did things that led me to believe he loved me too. I kept feeling more ill and getting weaker than ever. I went to the doctor, but the medication he prescribed never helped. I started coughing up blood. Marie took me to another doctor. He took one look at me, weighed me, then told Marie to take me immediately to the tuberculosis hospital on the southeastern coast of Florida. After getting there, we started walking toward the hospital, but I collapsed on the pavement. Marie grabbed me up in her arms and ran with me. A nurse saw us and rushed out of the hospital with a wheelchair.

After my examination, I was diagnosed with tuberculosis. The doctor told me and Marie that if she hadn't brought me in when she did, I would have died. While I was in the hospital, my bowels locked up, and the doctor tried pumping my stomach, hoping he wouldn't have to operate. It looked like a jungle of tubes were hooked up to me. Mom was called, and Marie called Landon to come home from his long-distance job. When he came to see me, there were tears in his eyes and he looked worried, so once again I felt loved.

K, Mom, and Margarete came down from Kentucky, picked Aunt Rena from her home, and continued down to see me. By then, I had recovered without an operation. We had a heartwarming visit. It was sad to say goodbye, but they had to go home once they knew I was going to be okay.

I often thought about my friends, and Landon brought Anne to see me. Marie and Tim watched Brianna for the entire seven months that I was in the hospital. Marie loved Brianna dearly. Brianna was especially close to her Granny Marie. Although Marie and I had a few differences between us, as most in-laws do, we still cared about each other. I thought of her as my second mother.

After I was discharged, Landon took me with him on the trips for his job. We went to Canada; it was nearly Christmas. We went shopping, and Landon bought Brianna a red velvet dress that I had picked out. After getting back home, he went on another monthlong trip. When he came home, he told me to go to the doctor for treatment because he had a venereal disease. I went and received the treatment that was needed. Even after that, Landon never slowed down when it came to infidelity. Nothing mattered to him but women. Maybe that's where I fit into his life—I was a woman.

Caleb had been sent to a juvenile holding facility for a short time. He was later sent to a reform school in south-central Florida, and he escaped with a friend he met there. They somehow got stranded in a very swampy area that they knew nothing about. They took off on foot in the snake-infested swamp, where they found an old, abandoned, burned-out car they used for shelter for two days. Very hungry and thirsty, they tried to find their way out. Caleb knew the swamp water could make him deathly ill, but his thirst wouldn't let him pass it up. He drank the water, and surprisingly it didn't make him sick They didn't know how deep the swamp was in case they had to make a quick getaway if there were snakes or gators nearby.

Caleb felt a strange feeling come into his heart as though someone were telling him there was a shallow place further down from them. Caleb led the way further down and told his buddy as he pointed, "This is where we can cross." Just as he felt it would be, it was shallow. When they made it to the open field, they were caught by the rangers. Caleb said that was the first time he was glad he got caught. After he was released, he got into more trouble and was sent to jail.

Connie and her husband, Ray, moved back to Florida from Georgia, and they and Daddy visited Caleb in jail. A few days later, Connie, her husband, and I went back and visited Caleb. When a guard was searching Connie's purse, I made an off-the-wall comment to him about wishing Caleb wasn't in jail. The guard said he did too because since Caleb had been in there, he had set his cell on fire and torn up the ceiling. Once the guard was done searching Connie's purse, we were allowed in to visit my brother.

While I was talking to Caleb, I kept hearing a pecking noise. When I looked in the next cell, I saw Daddy. When I asked him what he was doing there, he said he was accused of sneaking Caleb a hacksaw. Connie already knew that Daddy was there. When I asked her if Daddy had done that, she said yes. Several months later, Daddy was released. Several months after that, Caleb was also released.

CHAPTER 26

In 1971, Connie and Ray divorced, that was also the year that Mom and K's last child, Larry, was born. I started going to church with Aunt Rena and got saved. Being forgiven of my sins felt so great! It was a major turnaround for me. I even portrayed an angel in our Christmas play that year. Landon took me on a long-distance trip. He said that he had to get some pills that would keep him awake, and the only place to get them was at a cathouse. So he stopped at a cathouse and went in. I was afraid to hitchhike, so I sat in the big rig, feeling lower than a snake. When Landon came out of the cathouse, we went on our merry way. After we came home, my brother brought his girlfriend down from Tennessee and moved in with Landon, Daddy, and me. Caleb fixed himself and his girlfriend a bed in a small area between my bedroom and the bathroom. Daddy slept on the couch. She and I became friends. I babysat her small children for her while she worked in a packinghouse. Caleb had been in the city jail, but he had escaped and was hiding in my apartment. He was eventually caught and sent back.

Marie and Tim were partners as long-distance truck drivers, and Landon, Brianna, and I moved in with them. But my daddy stayed put. I really don't remember where Caleb and his girlfriend moved to. There was a time when Landon would come home from his long-distance trips, throw a quarter on our bed, and tell me to go out with other men and have fun. I didn't think he could degrade me anymore than he had in the past, but that brought my self-esteem even lower. Even if it had been a $1,000, he knew I wouldn't go. I was faithful for most our marriage, and all of it as far as he knew, so he just wanted to brag to his friends that I was a faithful wife. When he put his friends up to asking me out and they told him I refused them, which was true, it boosted his ego tremendously.

Women commonly drove by our home, yelling for Landon to come out with them. They phoned, but when I answered, they hung up. I knew it was Landon's women because of the background noise. Landon denied the affairs, saying they were only trying to break us up. The ones he didn't deny, he shrugged off as jokes or begged me to take him back when we separated because of them. Whether I went to church or not, nothing seemed to matter to him except other women and his pride.

There were times when Landon came home and woke me up with a kiss, telling me that he loved me. He said when he was on his trips and the song "Kiss an Angel Good Morning" played, he thought of me, and that became his song from him to me. I, on the other hand, kept thinking of the song "Your Good Girl's a Gonna Go Bad." I was fighting that thought but getting weaker. More than once, Anne would tell me that Landon was out with other women. She got mad at me for taking Landon's abuse. She had never seen me put up with abuse from anyone until I got married. I believe she would have beaten him up if she could.

One of Landon's affairs included Anne's husband, Stan. We found them in another small town at a gas station about four miles from my hometown. I didn't know Landon's date. He and Stan were outside of Landon's car, and the girls stayed inside the car. When the girls saw us coming, they jumped out and ran through the sugarcane field. It was night and I don't know how they made it home safely. There were snakes, and an actual gator was known to be in the fields. I was too hurt to speak; nevertheless, Landon snapped at me, telling me not to say a word.

Anne was so mad, she jumped in her car to ram Landon's. She put the pedal to the metal, but the brakes stuck, which kept everyone from getting blown to pieces. At the time, I didn't understand the full meaning of the protecting hand of God, but it had to be him who spared us that night. Anne left with Stan, and I left with Landon.

My hurt was wearing off, and I argued with Landon. After things calmed down, I asked Landon if he would teach me how to drive, but he refused. I wanted to get a job as I had at other times, but he denied me that as well. Marie and Tim were also against me working.

I thought of how I was being unfairly treated when Marie and Tim went along with Landon concerning different situations, and I thought of the past when Tim and Marie moved to Tennessee and Landon moved me and Brianna up there. Landon's plan was for me and Brianna to stay with his parents and for him to go back to Florida so that he could continue his cheating without any interference. But then it made me feel good when Tim didn't go along with Landon concerning this situation. Instead, Tim got angry at Landon, grabbed a butcher knife, and chased him through the woods.

Landon snuck back, got his car, and then he went back to Florida once again.

Landon told me once that if one set of parents didn't let him have his way, the other ones would, and he laughed. Anne would still get mad at me for reconciling with Landon every time, but as usual I did it anyway.

I didn't go on Landon's trips much, but the next one was to Texas. I wondered if he would make another cathouse stop and, if so, how I would handle it this time. We made it without any embarrassing stops. While coming home, Landon was driving on an interstate overpass, and the traffic was very heavy. As Landon was going around a curve too fast, he got too close to the edge. I felt my side of the tires leave the highway. We were beginning to flip over onto the traffic below. Suddenly, I felt as though a hand smoothly pulled the semi back on to the highway. That experience is hard to explain, but the feeling was peaceful. For Landon, it was different; he had to pull over as soon as he could. When he stopped, we stayed there quite a while until his nerves calmed down.

I believe the Lord had compassion for us and took care of us. I learned from a personal relationship with the Lord that he is full of compassion, for the Bible says in Psalm 111:4, "He hath made his wonderful works to be remembered: The Lord is gracious and full of compassion." Another experience concerning the Lord happened while I was in my church. The Lord manifested his spirit in color. I thought I was the only one who saw it, but after it disappeared, one of the sisters in Christ asked if anyone saw it. When the rest of us said yes, we talked about the amazing sight and blessed privilege the Lord gave us to behold his beauty.

Marie and Tim had become long-distance truckers before Landon. While they and Landon were gone, there was nothing much for me and Brianna to do, so we often watched TV while eating boiled peanuts. Brianna loved to watch *Lassie*. One episode was sad, and Brianna cried. When I told Landon, he brought her a female Collie puppy home from Miami, which surprised me. Brianna's little eyes seemed to glow, and her face lit up when she was with her puppy. She named the puppy Sugar. Sugar was a good watchdog most of the time. She followed me when I rode Brianna around in the trailer park on my bike, which Brianna enjoyed.

Brianna also enjoyed it when she and I colored pictures from her book. Brianna loved water as much as I did. She didn't have a pool, so I let her play in the bathtub. When I had things to do, I left her in the water with what seemed to her a tub full of toys. She sang her little heart out. When she stopped, I checked on her. I wanted to buy her more toys, but I had no money of my own. Landon wouldn't buy her much of anything unless Marie made him. When Brianna was first born, he hadn't bought her anything at all.

CHAPTER 27

On one of Landon's trips to Mississippi, he stopped at the home of one of Joni's nieces and wound up getting her pregnant. He spent that Christmas with her instead of with me and Brianna. He called me from her home, telling me that his truck broke down and that he had to stay with it at his job site.

This brought me to the point of quitting church again instead of holding on to my faith. Because of that, when another guy asked me out, I went. It wasn't revenge this time—I was just plain tired. Landon came home and found out about my affair. He tricked me into telling him who I went out with. We got into an argument, and I told him, "This is what you wanted me to do all along." Landon started slapping me. He left to find the guy that I went out with. When he did, he tried to fight him, but the other guy held him down. When he finally let Landon up, Landon came to finish it up with me. The other guy and some of our friends came to Marie and Tim's mobile home. Landon threw me out of the house and got me on the ground and choked me until I started blacking out. Our friend George pulled Landon off me. I believe if George hadn't helped me, Landon would have killed me.

I tried to get some things and Brianna from the house,

but Landon wouldn't let me. Some of our friends took me to Daddy's. This time Marie told Landon to apologize to me and bring me home. He did and, of course, I went back to him. Because George helped me that night, Landon accused me of sleeping with George.

Landon suggested that I visit Grandma and Grandpa Crawley. He said he would take me, so I wouldn't have to ride a bus. When he got to the edge of town where my grandparents lived, he put me and Brianna out of his semi and told me to call a cab. Landon had been to Grandma's before. He knew it was still about twenty miles up the mountain. He gave me some money, but he didn't know how much the cab would cost. He didn't even wait to see if a cab would show up. He just drove off, leaving me and his five-and-a-half-year-old daughter standing on the side of the road at a phone booth. I thank the Lord that a criminal didn't try to harm us. I got a cab and Grandpa had to finish paying the fare. A couple of weeks later, Grandpa paid my bus fare back home. When Landon heard that I was back, sure enough, we reconciled again.

On Landon's next trip, he had stayed gone for a few weeks. When he came home, he asked me if I would help him raise his baby boy because the mother of the child was giving him up for adoption. Although it came as no surprise and it was heartache for me, I said yes. When Landon went on a long trip and I was washing dishes, I thought about the entire devastating trauma Landon put me and Brianna through, even the ones I haven't written about. I also thought, *Alice, why don't you go ahead and get the divorce you have thought about and get one big hurt over with instead of constantly getting hurt?* The importance of Brianna being raised by both parents had left me. And I finally realized that my love for him wasn't enough, and I was extremely tired of trying to hold on to a marriage that just wasn't working. Choking back my tears, I packed Brianna's and my clothes and left. Brianna and I stayed with Caleb. I finally filed for a divorce and got a job at a local fast-food restaurant near Caleb's home. When Landon came home from his trip and found Brianna and I gone, he came looking for me. He found me riding around with Anne. He stopped us and cursed me, and I cursed him back.

CHAPTER 28

Around the same time that I was finally getting tired of Landon's lies, my friend Lizz and her sister, Becky, had a horrible experience. Lizz married Lucas Lawson not long after my marriage to Landon. When Lizz and Becky started working in a liquor store, Lucas told Lizz to watch out for anyone who came into the store wearing a long trench coat because she would get robbed. You never know what might happen.

One night while Becky and Lizz were getting ready to close the store, a man came in wearing one of those coats. Lizz was leaving before Becky. Becky told Lizz to stick around because she felt something wasn't right, so Lizz stayed.

The man grabbed Lizz around her neck, pulled out his sawed-off shotgun, pointed it at Lizz's head, and told Becky if she pushed the alarm, he would shoot Lizz. He made Becky give him the money from the register. Then he put Lizz and Becky in the back room. Lizz said that all she could think was, *Oh God, I'm gonna die.* She was terrified. Suddenly, a man pulled up to the drive-through window to give his order, causing the robber to panic and run out of the store. Lizz never worked there again. Lizz said she believed the robber had intended to shoot her and Becky. Lizz and her family thank the Lord for sparing Becky's and her life, and so do I. Lizz and Lucas have always treated me like part of their family, and she and Lucas have a beautiful family of their own to enjoy.

CHAPTER 29

I had finally decided to start dating again when Lou asked me if he could keep Brianna for a few days, so I let him. As I was getting ready to meet my date, Landon showed up. He got on his knees in the dirt, begging me to take him back, and I refused. Then he said Brianna was crying because she wanted to see me. I didn't believe him, but he kept on. I agreed to see her, and he promised to take me and then bring me back.

After getting in his semi and heading out, he passed Lou's street, and I argued with him. He was crying and pleading for me to give him another chance. He threatened to kill himself if I didn't take him back. He wanted me to go to Georgia with him. I had grown very weary of his crying. All I wanted him to do was shut up. I told him I would go, and he stopped crying.

When we got to Marie's home to pick up his clothes, I stayed in the truck. Marie came out and fussed at me, saying if Landon kills himself, it would be my fault. After I told her I was going with him, she calmed down and went inside her home. As Landon and I were on our way to Georgia, he said that if I didn't want to reconcile with him when we got home, he wouldn't bother me anymore.

After getting back home, I moved in with Daddy, and Landon left me alone. I believe Dad seeing Landon's abusiveness toward me finally caused him to realize just how much his past abuse toward Mom had hurt her. I had never seen such deep regret from Daddy—so much so that he cried!

My divorce became final in late 1973. Although I felt like a bird set free, I cried for years because of our divorce and Landon's abusiveness. It was around that year that a male acquaintance, who I don't recall, made fun of me for calling my daddy "Daddy" and said I should call him dad.

Caleb married Mia, and I moved in with them. The Kentucky Fried Chicken wasn't far from Caleb and Mia's, so I got a job there, and it didn't take me long to walk to and from work. After a few weeks of working and staying home, Caleb suggested that I go out and have some fun and that he would watch Brianna for me. When he told me that, he didn't mean for me to go wild, but that's what I did. Dad and I moved back to south-central Florida. We started working on a sod farm. Dad, Caleb, and I lived with one another off and on for a long time. Caleb and Mia, with their small daughter, Stacy, and son, Stephen, moved in with us some time in 1975.

Caleb, Dad, and I started working on the sod farm together, and I started back to church. At that point, my ex-boyfriend Stanly came back into my life. We dated for a short time, and then he asked me to marry him. I felt like I had died and gone to heaven.

I never hesitated to say yes. He said that he lived in Georgia and that he had to go back to work, but he would send for me and then he left. I came back to earth with the thought, *He's leaving me again. How long this time?* I was hurt once more, so I went to Mom's in Kentucky. When I came back, I lived with Dad and Caleb again.

Although I lived within walking distance from town, I

felt it was past time for me to learn how to drive. I asked Caleb if he would teach me. I knew he would be the best one for the job. He would be patient. He wasn't afraid of anything, at least until he got in the car with me. I was following his instructions fine. As he was teaching me to back up, I was going too slow for him. He told me to go a little faster, so I obeyed, but I kept speeding up until we were going much too fast. When he saw that I wasn't going to slow down, he yelled for me to hit the brake. I panicked and hit the brakes so hard that we started doing donuts backward. We were glad the traffic was light. We ended up in a resident's yard and tore it up. Caleb told me to hurry and get away from there. After we left, he said my lesson for the day was over. Not much later, I passed my driver's test and got my license, believe it or not!

Dad bought me a used red Mustang. I thought it was the most beautiful thing I had ever owned, even if it looked like it was ready to fall apart. I was a fast driver. Dad said he didn't want to be standing on the side of the road when I drove by. He was afraid that a piece of car would fly off and knock him out. We all cracked up.

CHAPTER 30

My sister Connie had started living with a divorcée named Jose Martinez. One night in 1974, Jose, his fourteen-year-old son, Renan, Connie, and her seven-year-old son, Sean, were on their way back to their home from visiting Jose's father, who lived a few towns over from them.

Connie hadn't been driving her new standard pickup long. She was very nervous about driving near a canal and on such a narrow, curvy road. She was driving slowly but decided to pick up some speed. Just as she got into third gear, she started having a hard time keeping the truck under control. She swerved, causing the truck to go over the bank. It flipped upside down in the canal. Jose and Sean were in the back of the camper. Connie went into shock. Even though the horn was steadily blowing, she felt an eerie silence. Everything seemed to get very still, even while the wheels were spinning.

The water rushed over her head, reviving her. She panicked as she brought her head up out of the water. When the water was up to her neck, all she could think was, *Oh God, I'm going to die.* About that time, something touched her leg. She started screaming, thinking it was a gator, but it was Renan trying to find her in the murky water. When he found her, she was terrified. He tried to calm her down. Jose kicked out the camper glass and escaped with Sean. Then Jose helped Connie and Renan to safety. A nearby resident heard the truck horn constantly blowing and called for help. An officer and a reporter came. The truck was a total loss, and the accident was put in the paper, which Connie kept for years.

I don't know why my cousin Roy wasn't called to the accident. He worked at a wrecker company, rescuing victims from canals. He said it was a dangerous and terrifying job, but he loved it. Connie said the accident left her with such frightful memories. She thanks God for sparing her and her loved ones.

CHAPTER 31

Mom and K took my five youngest siblings with them to Tennessee to visit Grandma Crawley. Mom let ten-year-old Nae and eight-year-old Micah go with Uncle Sut and his son to a resort park not far away. It had a swinging bridge and a nice swimming area, among other wonderful sights.

Micah and Nae waded toward the falls. As the water became swifter, Micah went back to the shore. Nae kept wading and, not realizing how close she was getting to the falls, she slipped. She said she was probably carried a hundred feet from the falls, but it seemed to her that maybe she was carried fifty feet. Whether a hundred or fifty feet, to a ten-year-old staring death in the face, it was terrifying. Nae grabbed hold of a rock and held on for dear life. When Uncle Sut saw the danger that she was in, he rushed to save her. He finally managed to pull her to safety just in the nick of time because she was getting too weak to hold on. The rock was just too big for her small hands.

I would have liked to learn more about Uncle Sut's feelings concerning the situation, but I didn't think to ask at that time. Now it's too late to ask Uncle Sut because he passed away. It has been told that people have plunged to their deaths from going over that falls.

CHAPTER 32

Back down to Florida we went! School was out for the summer, so Landon asked me if Brianna could spend the summer with him. He led me to believe he still lived in Florida. He said he would bring her back when school started. I believed him, because I thought he was happily married. His wife was a young, pretty girl named Karen, and they were going to have a baby. I hadn't heard of him being forced into marring her. Therefore, I believed he had no reason to feel threatened into a marriage. Since the judge awarded me full custody of Brianna, I thought he had to bring her back regardless, so I let her go. When our divorce was final, I never thought to ask the judge or my attorney any of these questions, and they never volunteered to explain them to me. They must have thought I knew.

School started, but no Brianna. I got worried and mad at the same time. In my heart, I knew Landon had done it to me again. Landon's cousin, Sharon, and I were friends. She secretly told me that Landon had moved Brianna to a town in Texas.

I rushed to explain the situation to my attorney. He explained to me that it wasn't considered kidnapping, since I had given my permission for her go, and I would have to bring her back myself.

Uncle Roland, Aunt Barbara, and Uncle Jonathan had moved to Texas during the sixties. Uncle Jonathan was visiting Grandma Crawley, and they came down to visit Aunt Rena in Florida. I told Aunt Rena what Landon had done. When she told Uncle Jonathan, he said he would take me to Texas after he took Grandma back home to Tennessee. After taking Grandma home, we went to Texas, and I could hardly wait. After getting there, he took me to Uncle Roland and Aunt Barbara's, where I mostly stayed. We didn't know if Landon had a phone, so Aunt Barbara searched the phone book, and what a joy I felt when his name and address were in there. I called, hoping he was still there, but when he answered, I hung up.

Aunt Barbara and I headed to where Landon was. He lived across from the school where Karen had enrolled Brianna. We parked in the school's parking lot. I disguised myself and watched through the rearview mirror as Karen walked Brianna to school. I thought my heart would fall to the floorboard.

I thought I saw which room Karen took Brianna into, but I was not sure, so as soon as Karen went inside her home, Aunt Barbara and I jumped out of her car and had to search the classrooms until we found Brianna. Not thinking of my actions, I walked in and grabbed Brianna's arm. When the teacher saw me, she rushed to Brianna's rescue. I explained to the teacher what Landon had done. The principal was called. I repeated the story to him. He said he wasn't allowed to let me have Brianna, but that he would keep her there, and I needed to get an attorney. I didn't have much time, because school was about to let out for the day, so Aunt Barbara and I quickly found one. I explained to the attorney the entire situation. He said I could place Brianna in a children's facility until he got the paperwork ready for court, or I could take a chance and let her go to her dad's. But if he took her out of the state, there was nothing anyone could do. I chose the children's facility. It broke my heart to leave her there. She looked so lost and pitiful. She was too young to understand, so I just gave her a see-you-later kiss and told her I would be back.

Fortunately, it didn't take long until court day. The judge got mad at Landon after I told him I never tried to keep Brianna from him. The judge gave Brianna back to me. It was a blessing that Landon had to pay for everything, because I didn't have any money. Aunt Barbara and Uncle Roland paid my bus fare home. This was the very important role that Uncle Roland, Aunt Barbara, and Uncle Jonathan played in my life that I have always been grateful for. Thanks from the bottom of my heart!

Brianna and I were on our way home from Uncle Roland, Aunt Barbara, and Uncle Jonathon when we had a layover in Mississippi because a hurricane was headed our way.

While I was in the bus station, a guy named Landon (of all names) asked me out, and I refused. His name alone sickened me. I was tired of buses, but I was glad to get back on that one.

Not long after I got home, Marie asked me if she could take Brianna back to Texas to visit. I agreed only if she signed a legal document promising to bring Brianna back at my appointed time. It hurt her feelings that I asked such a thing, because she was so used to me always giving in to them; nevertheless, she signed it. That ended the kidnapping problem. No matter what the law says, I call that kidnapping!

CHAPTER 33

I enrolled Brianna in school, and things seemed to be going well for her. I was laid off at the sod farm and became discouraged and lonely. Instead of holding on to the Lord for strength, I let go again. I started drinking more that time than ever. I even smoked more pot.

Caleb asked me to go camping with him, Mia, our cousin Jamie, our friend Todd, and a few others. I let Brianna stay with her grandpa Lou, and then I went camping.

Caleb and Todd fixed a fire to cook gator stew and then they and Jamie went hunting for one. When they spotted a gator, Jamie thought he would play Tarzan. He said he would go in after it if Todd shot it. Todd shot it, but Jamie didn't feel like Tarzan any longer and went back on his word, so Todd pushed Jamie into the water where the gator went down. Todd and Caleb laughed so hard at such a funny sight.

Caleb said he didn't believe a rocket could have come straight up any faster than Jamie did. Jamie was scared, swinging his arms, and fist-fighting mad. That sight caused Caleb and Todd to laugh even harder.

Todd was determined to have gator stew, so he jumped in after it, but he found out quickly that it was still alive. Todd wrestled it to the bank. We had a fine stew. Later Caleb told me the gator wasn't all we ate. I asked him what else was put in the stew, but he wouldn't say. As I think about it, I still don't want to know.

Todd introduced me to his drug of choice—pills. The pills made me sick, so I stuck with drinking and pot for a while before trying anything else in pill form.

CHAPTER 34

Carol and I went to Kentucky to visit our families. I never took drugs or alcohol around Mom and K. I knew it was a wise choice to respect their Christianity and their home, so Carol dropped my clean self off at Mom's and then she went to visit her family.

After a short visit, Carol picked me up to go riding with her, her boyfriend, Maxwell, and her brother, Edward. It was snowing, and it seemed as though it was an exceptionally freezing winter, but we didn't care.

We were drinking and ended up on a mountain that I thought the Kentucky mountain boys knew about. Maxwell was drunk and unable to drive any further, so he parked for the night. We all shared a blanket and talked until we fell asleep.

The next morning, when we awoke, there was quite a bit more snow on the ground than we cared for, and we were surprised to find ourselves on a very narrow road and dangerously close to a cliff. We wondered how in the world we survived getting up there and how were we going to get down with the cliff on one side and the mountain wall with a small ditch on the other side.

The guys knew the only option was to slide the two left

tires in the ditch and drive the car down backward very slowly and carefully, so that's how we made it down. Carol and I were glad to be back in our families' homes. It's amazing we didn't freeze to death. We weren't dressed for that bitter night. The next day, Carol and I went back to Florida.

I was hired back at the same sod farm that I had worked at before. I felt our boss, Jamison, was good to all his workers. I enjoyed working for him, but my drinking caused me to be unable to work, so I quit. I had been sinking into a deep state of depression. My body was getting very weak, and I was losing weight.

One night, while I was in a bar, Jamison and his mother-in-law, who was called Big Janie, were there. She had been accusing me of having an affair with him. I was tired of hearing it because it wasn't true, so I deliberately provoked her to hit me. I figured after that, she would leave me alone, and she did. Afterward, I saw her again, and she was friendly. I felt overall that she was a good person.

Dad was keeping Brianna's collie, Sugar, for us. Landon knew Brianna loved Sugar, but he didn't care; he just came one day and took her away. To this day, we don't know what happened to that poor dog.

In 1976, Connie and Jose had their first child, Cassandra. It was around that time that I started smoking more pot and taking speed along with it (but I never had to get it at a cathouse!).

CHAPTER 35

While I was still messing up my life, Caleb was pulling crazy stunts with his friends, like hunting gators. After one was found, his friend Baxter shot it and went in the water to bring it out. To his surprise, it wasn't dead, but Baxter wasn't going to be defeated. The gator almost won. It battered and bloodied Baxter up pretty good, but with help, the gator was finally taken out of the water, put in a van, and taken to a home near town. The guys put the gator in the bathroom and told their wives to look inside. Wondering what was going on, and as skeptical as the wives were, they looked in the bathroom and saw the gator. Before they could say anything, the gator got lose. The wives screamed as they ran, knocking over furniture on their way out of the home, where the guys were standing around laughing. The guys were too drunk to realize how dangerous it could have been.

Caleb and Mia divorced, and Mia eventually left, taking her two small children out of Florida. After a while, Caleb started dating a girl named Babbie, who had moved down from Ohio with her family before Mia left. In 1977, Babbie gave birth to their daughter, Vanessa, while I was getting to the point where I didn't care what I did.

I feel it's time for me to let some of my old acquaintances

and closest friends know why I did the things I did—because of Landon's abusiveness toward me and Brianna. I knew I was ruining my reputation big time with beer, wine, drugs, sex, and dressing very trashy. But more of that will be revealed in my daughter, Brianna's stories toward the end of the book. We'll just say for now that I did things I truly regret and allowed sin to take me further than I wanted to go. I didn't have the willpower to get out of my situation on my own. If I could undo the terrible things I did, I truly would.

CHAPTER 36

Still getting more depressed as time went on, I tried different drugs. I even thought of trying cocaine and heroin, but for some reason I steered away from them. Everything was taking a toll on my body—there were times when I even felt my heart stop. I could hardly hold myself up. I looked like a hundred-year-old walking skeleton, but I continued ruining my health and reputation, still not realizing or caring about the seriousness of it all.

In 1979, Caleb and Babbie got married. She loved Caleb very much and he loved her. Babbie said it broke her heart every time she heard Caleb cry, longing to see his children. I have seen the hurt on Caleb's face and heard it in his voice when he told me how much he wanted to see them. Babbie used to watch them for Caleb while he worked, before Mia took them completely away. Babbie treated them as though they were her own children. Caleb and Babbie tried different ways to find them. They even talked about hiring an investigator, but they couldn't because their funds were very limited. Babbie is more than a sister in-law to me; she is one of my best friends!

Caleb had straightened up some and tried to get me to pull my life together, but I wouldn't listen. I rented a long tin shed that had been converted into a home. It stuck out like a sore thumb. It had a brick bathroom without a door, so I had to hang a blanket up to use for a door. The home wasn't much to look at, but it didn't bother me, considering the places I had lived in. It was home to Brianna and me. I had a full-size bed in the living room and a small cot in my kitchen. I slept on the cot when I was alone.

CHAPTER 37

My friend Sam came to see me. My ex-boyfriend Raymond came back into my life. They both tried to help me, but neither one of them could, because I had become too wild and uncontrollable with my depressed emotions. They couldn't reach me any more than my family could. Caleb, Dad, and Connie checked on me occasionally.

Joni's brother, Wade, had moved back from Michigan and married my girlfriend They were my neighbors. They babysat Brianna for me while I went to bars. My neighbor who lived in a two-story apartment upstairs also babysat for me while I went to bars. The upstairs neighbor's kids and my daughter played together.

I didn't consider myself as an abusive mother for a long time, because I still played with Brianna. I never beat her. But there were times I didn't feed her properly. I left her home alone twice when she was eleven years old. I even ignored a red flag when Brianna cried because she stopped wanting to go to her Grandpa Lou's house, and that made me a neglectful, dangerous, and abusive mother.

I'm writing this with blurred vision from tears. I got so wrapped up in my wild life that I had become more thoughtless than Landon. It's extremely hard for me to think about the way I treated Brianna.

CHAPTER 38

Although my thoughts would go back to the good times when Brianna and I went to church, I couldn't shake the way Landon treated us and the awful things he used to say to me while we were married. He said, "No one will ever love you or want you but me." He said it so often that I ended up believing him. I choose not to tell the worst things he has said to me. Anyway, after Stanly left me that last time to go to Georgia and I left church and went wild again, Landon's seemed to take control of me, and I started to take advantage of men. I believed they were out to take advantage of me, so why shouldn't I take advantage of them? I know there are a lot of good men in this world, but after I divorced Landon, I didn't believe it for a long time.

I fell into deeper depression. The pressures of life were getting the best of me. I thought of ending it all. Selfishness kicked in again. I knew my family would take care of Brianna. I let her spend the night with my upstairs neighbor, so she could have other kids to play with. One night, my friend Jane and I were to meet at the bar, but on my walk to the bar, I stopped at a convenience store and bought a bottle of sleeping pills, and then I went out to meet Jane. She didn't know what I was up to. I got drunk. I don't remember how I got home.

When I took the pills, it caused me to throw up. I felt faint as I reached for a small throw rug and covered my mess as I was blacking out on my cot.

In my mind, I saw myself crawling up my neighbor's flight of stairs, reaching for Brianna, trying to get to her and calling her name. As I crawled halfway up, I saw myself fall asleep.

Sometime that following day, Dad came to check on me. He didn't know what I had done, but he felt something wasn't right. He tried to wake me up, but I couldn't respond. He got worried, so he decided to take me to his apartment. He struggled to get me in his car.

After getting there, it was even a harder struggle for him to get me upstairs. He put me in his bed, where I slept for three days. For the most part of those three days, I didn't know I was in the world. However, during those days my mind was fading in and out. I could hear Dad talking to me, but I couldn't respond. I went back to sleep.

When Caleb came to Daddy's near the end of that third day, I regained a little strength. I could hear Dad tell Caleb that I had been sleeping much longer than normal and I still couldn't speak. Caleb tried walking me around, hoping I would wake up. My response was too weak, so he laid me back down. He told Dad that if I wasn't better soon, he was going to take me to the hospital.

Caleb got suspicious that I had tried to harm myself. When he went to my home to search for evidence, to his surprise, a car had run through my kitchen and over my cot where I had been sleeping after my suicide attempt. If Dad had not taken me to his apartment when he did, I believe that accident would have finished me off.

I was told the upstairs kids were in their parents' car with Brianna playing around and ran the car through my kitchen.

My home was a disaster! Caleb had a hard time searching through the rubbish trying to find what I took to harm myself. Finally, though, he found the empty pill bottle.

CHAPTER 39

Caleb returned to Dad's and stayed until I was more myself. Caleb sat on the bed and asked me what I had done, saying, "You tried to kill yourself, didn't you?" I could hear the fear in his voice. I was too choked up from seeing his hurt, even though I could speak, that I just looked at him silently. I'm glad I got better when I did. If I hadn't, Caleb and Daddy were going to take me to the hospital, and who knows what that would have led to once the hospital found out that it was a suicide attempt.

I thought about Grandma and sent her a box of candy with a letter inquiring about her health. Her caregiver sent me a couple of pictures of her along with a thank-you note, letting me know Grandma was doing fine. The last time Daddy saw Grandma, he cried. I thought he would like to have the pictures, so I gave them to him. When Dad visited some of his female cousins in Tennessee, he gave the pictures to them. Their families have always been good to Mom, Dad, and us kids. We all got along well and had love and respect for one another. I believe in giving honor where honor is due. I've been trying to do that throughout these stories. Still thinking about Grandma, I thought of the possibility of being insane. In other words, was I becoming mentally ill, the very thing

I had feared? I believe anyone who attempts suicide has a mental problem.

I know everyone has an appointed time to leave this world, but I praise the Lord for all the times he has spared my life thus far. I am alive to witness the Lord's great mercy and tell others that suicide is not the way out of any troublesome situation.

CHAPTER 40

By this time, I thought I could pick up the pieces of my shattered life on my own by staying out of bars, so I thought babysitting would help me. It sure was worth a try. So I babysat Jane's kids for her while she met her boyfriend, Stewart, at a bar. I had been tired of my wild life for such a long time. I thought of going back to church, but I couldn't seem to make the effort. Babysitting sounded like a solution, and I felt proud of myself for trying. Brianna and Jane's kids were best friends. Jane's daughter was a little older than my Brianna. Babysitting was going well. Bedtime came, and I lay down on the foldout couch in Jane's small one-bedroom trailer, so she could have her bed when she came home. Just as the kids fell asleep, there was a knock on the door. When I answered, it was Stewart.

I had known Stewart for a long time. He was one of my ex-boyfriends. He never gave me any reason to distrust him, so I let him in. He said Jane told him I was babysitting, so he came to check on me and the kids. Then he grabbed me, and the harshness of it totally blew my mind. I knew I was in trouble. I fought with him in a whisper for the kids' sake, begging him to leave. After he got what he came for, he left. I was devastated and wanted to report it. But who would have believed me with my terrible reputation? Maybe I would have been blamed—I didn't want to chance it in court, so I left it alone and went back to the bars.

CHAPTER 41

Caleb quit the sod farm and worked in a tree business, trimming and cutting them down. It was a dangerous job. It put him in some very dangerous situations, but he loved his job and was making more money.

He bought a fifteen-foot runabout boat. One beautiful day, he and I went riding in it. We were slowly cruising around. It helped ease my mind. We were drinking, talking, and laughing, when all of a sudden, a huge gator surfaced, causing me and Caleb to jump toward each other. We had seen many gators in our lives, but that was the largest ever. Curious, Caleb wanted to take a closer look. As quietly as possible, we got closer than I cared to, and then it went under. Caleb wanted to stay longer, but after thinking it might turn us over, we went home.

A few days later, Daddy, Jane, and I took Caleb's boat to the spot where we saw the monstrous gator because Dad was hoping to see it too. We three were drinking, but Dad didn't know Jane and I had been taking speed earlier that day. It was getting late into the evening, and I wanted to take a dip. Dad asked me not to, but I wouldn't listen. I told Dad I would be all right. I eased into the water, holding on to the side bar. After a few minutes, I started getting weak and started slipping away, but I was able to grab the bar. Feeling uneasy, knowing I was unable to swim, and thinking about that monster, I asked Daddy to help me back inside the boat. He did and then he took me home. He didn't want me to try another stupid stunt.

CHAPTER 42

One night, while I was in a bar, my old school friend Ricky showed up. I hadn't seen him in years. We dated occasionally, then he met a girl named June, and they started living together. Dad and I moved into a duplex next to them. Connie and Jose lived about a block away. I was still in a deep state of depression. I went to the bar, where I joined some friends. We agreed to go to the beach and return home before daylight. Brianna and Dad were asleep, so I believed it would be all right. On our way to the beach, we stopped at a friend's home and continued drinking and spent the night. The next day I told them I wanted to go home, but they stayed and partied some more.

On the third day, I intended to hitchhike if they didn't take me home. I was missing Brianna and wanted to be with her, believe it or not. Also, I knew Connie and Daddy would be worried about me. I told Anne's ex-husband, Stan, that Connie would report me missing.

My depression, worry, and tears started showing, and they took me home. I knew they hadn't meant any harm and we remained friends. When I got home, Daddy was at work, so I walked to Connie's, hoping Brianna was there. As I was walking up her driveway, she was coming out of her home with my picture, headed for the police station. When I saw her coming toward me, I could see fear and anger mixed. Brianna ran and grabbed me and was holding on like glue. After I explained to Connie my situation, she was relieved and calmed down. I'm sure glad her relief won over her anger. It's what kept her from flattening me out like a pancake. I was flat enough as it was.

Another night, I got drunk at a neighbor's home instead of a bar. I knew it was time for me to go home, so I started walking. Because of my blurred vision and it being pretty dark, I staggered into a tall cactus and filled my shoulder full of stickers. It was hard enough to pick them out sober, let alone drunk. It took weeks for my shoulder to heal.

Another night while, I was at a bar dancing, Lizz and Lucas were sitting nearby. Lizz and I were lit. She yelled, "We can whip everyone in here, can't we, Alice?" I yelled back, "Sure we can." No one took us up on it, and the band played on. Now I'm thankful that people ignored us. I probably would have been splattered, but I would have given it my best to win.

One day June asked me if I would take care of her small son, Daniel, if anything ever happened to her. I said yes. She knew I had fallen in love with him; he was such a little sweetheart. On another occasion, she asked me if I would go with her to meet a guy she was cheating on Ricky with, and I did.

CHAPTER 43

In 1979, I moved back to south-central Florida and lived in the apartment downstairs from the previous home. Jane and I continued to go to bars together and talk about our abusive marriages. Other than Jane, I tried to hide my feelings from people by dancing, laughing, and pretending to have a good time. My thoughts would go back to church. I thought about church even when I was at drug parties. Church was the only peaceful place I had ever been, but I still made no effort to return.

Time passed, and then came the breaking point for me, which was another rape. I felt my whole world was crashing down on me. I knew if I didn't get help, I wouldn't be here much longer. I knew I needed help that could only come from the Lord. My attention also focused deeper on my family. I had not only shattered Brianna's and my life, but the rest of my family. They stopped coming around me. The week after the rape, on a Saturday while Brianna was outside playing and I was sitting on my couch, I thought how I was ruining Brianna's life and her trust in me—poor Brianna.! Nothing was getting better, only worse. I felt like the Prodigal Son and thought, *I know what I will do. I will go back to my Father's house, where I had it made.* The Bible says in Luke 15:13.

And not many days after the younger son gathered all together, and took his journey into a far country, and there wasted his substance with riotous living.

And he would fain have filled his belly with the husks that the swine did eat: and no man gave unto him.

And when he came to himself, he said, how many hired servants of my fathers have bread enough and to spare, and I perish with hunger!"

I will arise and go to my father, and will say unto him, Father; I have sinned against heaven, and before thee.

I was tired of wrestling with myself concerning church and my soul. I was finally ready to get back in church for good, no matter what! As I was thinking on the Lord, a sudden fear gripped my heart, and I wondered if the Lord would take me back after all I had done. It was about that time that two women came into the yard and asked Brianna if her mother was home. Brianna brought them to the door, and I invited them in. They invited Brianna and me to Sunday school. Brianna looked at me as if to say, *Please, Mommy, please.* I said to her, "If you will go to Sunday school in the morning, I will go to church with you Sunday night, Okay?" She said okay.

Sunday came, and Brianna went to Sunday school that morning on the church bus. Then it was my turn. I was afraid—although I wanted to go, I was changing my mind. Brianna looked at me with such sad disappointment, so I went to church with her.

We sat with Mrs. Phipps. I was terrified and nervous. When the altar call was given, Mrs. Phipps asked me if I wanted to go to the altar. I was too choked up to speak, so I nodded my head yes. She grabbed my arm tightly and almost ran me to the altar. I fell on my knees with tears that seemed to flow like a river, asking our heavenly Father for forgiveness in Jesus's name. I felt his forgiveness, and the burden of sin lifted off me, causing me to feel light as a feather and filled with an awesome peace. But I kept asking for his forgiveness. Finally, the Lord spoke to me through a sister in Christ through prophecy, saying, "I have forgiven you; now forgive yourself."

I'm glad our Father has no respect for person. He treated me like he treated the Prodigal Son. In the last part of the Bible verse in Luke 15:20, it says: "But when he was yet a great way off, his Father saw him, and had compassion, and ran, and fell on his neck and kissed him." Verse 24 says: "For this my son was dead and is alive again; he was lost and is found. And they began to be merry."

After getting home with Brianna, I asked her to forgive me for not being the mother she needed. We hugged, cried, and she forgave me, but forgiving myself has been one of the hardest tasks I have ever encountered, because the Lord is so good and doesn't deserve to be dishonored!

CHAPTER 44

Hurricane David was headed our way. By the time it reached us, it was downgraded to a category two. My home wasn't safe to stay in, so Caleb took me, Brianna, and my friend Rosemary to his home a little northeast of my hometown, where Dad and our friend Roberto were also.

We watched debris flying and falling everywhere, power lines falling and popping with sparks shooting all over the road. Caleb's driveway was a total mess. When everything died down, it looked safe enough to go home. As Brianna reached for Caleb's car door, a power line popped up and hit the car, missing Brianna by a few inches. I rushed her back inside Caleb's home. After a little more waiting, it was finally safe to go home. When we got home, Caleb and I were amazed to see my raggedy apartment still standing considering all the destruction that was around.

CHAPTER 45

Caleb and Babbie moved to a city on the eastern coast of Florida. Caleb had been drinking while he and Babbie were visiting their friends. When Caleb and Babbie returned home, Babbie was about to open the door of their home when Caleb pushed her away and grabbed up a snake that she was about to step on. Caleb was holding it too close to his face. It latched on to his nose. That made Caleb mad, and he started slapping it as though it were a person. After he pulled it loose, it latched on to his bottom lip. After struggling harder, he finally pulled it off his lip. The next morning, when he was sober, he checked himself to see if he was all right, then he went outside to find out what kind of snake it was. He was relieved to see it was a black snake. When I picture that event in my mind, I can see what a funny sight that was.

Caleb and Babbie met Richie, and they became friends. Caleb was planning a camping trip at the lake, and Richie asked him if he could go, so Caleb invited him along. Babbie came to invite me while Caleb went to invite our brother Micah and Daddy. While Babbie and I were on our way to the lake and the guys were setting up camp, a disaster struck in the form of an alligator.

Some of our friends came to the camp and took the small

boat and paddles to go joyriding, leaving Caleb with the larger boat without paddles.

Richie wanted to swim across the rim canal that circled the lake, which wasn't far from our old swimming area as young kids. Caleb, Dad and Micah told Richie not to go swimming because of the gators. Richie ignored them and dove in. He made it across to the other side with no problem. While on his way back, a gator surfaced and just stared at him. Not knowing how to handle the dangerous situation, Richie splashed water at it, thinking he would scare it away. Instead, it attacked him, pulling him under. Caleb, Dad, and Micah were bewildered, saying, "He's gone, he's gone." Just at that moment, Richie surfaced, then the gator surfaced and grabbed him again, taking him back under with water splashing extremely high. How Richie got loose was nothing short of a miracle.

Caleb yelled for Richie to go back to the bank and climb a tree. After Richie climbed a tree, he yelled at Caleb, telling him he was bleeding. Caleb, Dad, and Micah knew Richie was in desperate need of help. Dad's breathing was bad, leaving Caleb and Micah to handle the rescue. Caleb and Micah had no choice but to jump in the large boat and paddle with their hands. They managed to get Richie in the boat. As Caleb and Micah paddled halfway back, their friends showed up and helped put Richie in the small boat and back to camp. It was perfect timing, because Caleb and Micah were exhausted and didn't believe they could have made it to the camp and then to the hospital before Richie bled to death.

Babbie and I were almost at the camp when we met Caleb on his way to the hospital with Richie. The next day, Caleb and Babbie visited Richie at the hospital and gave him a stuffed gator for a souvenir. Caleb nicknamed Richie "Gator." Richie injuries were worse than they imagined. Not only was it a miracle that Richie escaped death, but as bad as his injuries were, it was a miracle he didn't lose any limbs. That incident was the conversation piece for the remainder of their stay at the camp. After Richie was discharged from the hospital, he went back to his home.

CHAPTER 46

Around 1980, Caleb and Babbie had another daughter that they named Violet. This was also the year when I moved in with my cousin Denny, his wife, Claire, and their baby son. June and Ricky had a son named Ricky. I'll call him little Ricky. June brought little Ricky to Denny's home to show him to me. Little Ricky was such a handsome baby. I enjoyed holding him while June and I talked. I asked about Daniel, June's son from a previous marriage. Ricky had adopted him. June and I talked a while longer and then she left with little Ricky.

In mid-1980, my sister Connie gave birth to her second daughter, Marisol. Connie had developed severe arthritis while she was working at a nearby restaurant. Her days started between two and three in the morning, and she would pace her floors in tears from the pain before clocking in at work at 5:00 a.m. It was hard on her, but she kept on working to support her small children. She was very excited about getting her income tax check that she was depending on to help her out. But Rosemary's and my friend Ralf stole it from Connie's mailbox. Connie was hurt and angry. I felt terrible for her loss because she needed it so much. I also felt bad for her because it was my friend who stole it. After Ralf was proven guilty in court, he got off with just a slap on the wrist, which was another blow to Connie. Nevertheless, she managed to continue working and supporting her children.

In 1981, Caleb and Babbie's last child, Berto, was born. Vanessa was pretty much a peaceful child like her Aunt Connie. Violet and Berto were more like their dad and I were, fighting each other to the max. This also was the year my sister Nae's daughter, Jasmine, was born. A year and a half later, her son, Jeremiah, was born.

When my only child, Brianna, and all my siblings' kids grew older, they became very respectful and polite adults. That's something we all learned as we grew older!

In 1982, my ex-boyfriend Stewart came back into my life, apologizing for his misconduct, and asked me to marry him. He had been married and divorced. I knew he couldn't break my heart, because I didn't love him. I learned a divorce wasn't hard to get. My wrong thoughts were if it didn't work out, I'd just get a divorce. Also, I'd show Landon that someone else did want me for a wife. I also thought if Stewart wanted to have a marriage with me and was willing to help me make it work, then I would give it another try. We talked about it, and he said he wanted it to work, so I told him I would marry him. I went to the department store where June worked to buy a nice dress. She and I talked for a little while, and then I left. Stewart and I got married in Hendry County, Florida. He went to church with me. It made me feel good to believe things would work out; instead, things went terribly wrong.

I worked for a dry-cleaning service, and Stewart would stop in occasionally to get money from me. It didn't bother me at first, but the habit became too great and I stopped giving it to him. Then he started helping himself to my money by going through my purse. I had started back to school but quit; I just couldn't handle that much pressure.

One night, Stewart made plans to go out. His mom asked me to go with him. Stewart and I went riding around, and he rode to a neighborhood to buy drugs around 1:00 a.m. I locked my door, concerned about my safety. After he got his drugs, he drove to a sugarcane field.

As he was unwrapping his cocaine, I thought of grabbing it and throwing it in the canal. Then I thought, *No, he might throw me in after it, and there's gators in there.* I thought of hitchhiking, but that was dangerous also. Then I told myself that if I made it home alive, I would get a divorce.

When Stewart had finished shooting up his drugs, he was unable to drive, so I got behind the wheel. As soon as I pulled onto the highway, an officer stopped me. He kept looking at Stewart and told me to get out of the car. He asked me several times if I was all right, and after repeating to him that I was, he let me go. As I was getting back in the car, I looked at the floorboard, and there was the drug wrapper near the gas pedal. I was glad the officer didn't spot it. If he had, I knew I would have gone to prison with Stewart. This was end our fifth month of marriage, and I filed for a divorce. It became final September 1982. I've seen people on TV shoot up drugs, but that was the first and last time that I had seen it in person. To me that is an awful sight.

I believe the Lord was the one who put the fear in my heart not to try cocaine and heroin back in my wild days. The Lord spares people from many different situations!

CHAPTER 47

In 1983, I moved back in with Denny and Claire. I got a job working in the meat department of a grocery store. I spent most of my spare time with Mr. and Mrs. Phipps. Mr. Phipps was a fire chief. He and Mrs. Phipps helped the Salvation Army at Christmas by giving toys to needy children. It was a joy to me when I helped. Mrs. Phipps was an inspiration to me. Her daughter, Caroline, and I became best friends when our children were young. The best times for me were when Caroline and I went to church together.

Mrs. Phipps and I enjoyed inviting people to church. I felt it was time for June to be invited, so I went to her workplace and invited her. She said, "Maybe someday." We talked a little while, and then I left. Three weeks later, Denny was reading the newspaper. He asked me, "Didn't you have a girlfriend named June?" I said, "Yes, I did," and then he handed me the newspaper. I read that she was found dead in a ditch where she had been for three weeks.

As I read, my eyes filled with tears. I became weak and sick to my stomach. I went to pay my respects to Ricky and their children. June and Ricky had been living in an apartment. The story was that June had gone alone to her brother's home in South Bay to a party. Around 2:00 a.m., she started hitchhiking back to her home. That was the last time she was seen alive. I won't go into detail about the condition in which she was found out of respect for her family, although they do know.

Ricky drove me to June's grave. As he lay beside her, he and I cried. On our way back to his parents' home, he kept crying and talking to me. He told me that he had had to take a polygraph test because he was a suspect in June's death. He told me that he had passed the test. He then asked me if I would move in with him and help him with his sons.

I told him I would help him out, but I would rather move back to where I was before. Ricky wanted us to have a husband-wife relationship, but I said no. I told him he needed to date other women for a while to find out what he really wanted. He kept begging and crying for me to stay, saying that he didn't want anyone else. He even threatened to kill himself if I didn't stay with him.

He knew I went to church, and he showed respect for that. I knew he drank some before June's death, but because of June's death, he drank more than usual. He said he would quit drinking if I would marry him. His drinking helped him cope with June's death. He asked me to have a little patience with him because of everything that had happened. My reluctance was leaving. Thinking about what others told me in the past about how all men were not alike, especially not like Landon, I thought surely I wouldn't be treated like that again.

I didn't know Ricky's complete nature, but as far as I knew, he was a hard worker, a good provider, and I had never known him to cheat on June. I felt in my heart he would hold to his word and stop drinking, so I gave marriage another chance.

In 1983, my sister Connie had her last child, Amber. She was very tiny, which earned her the nickname "Peanut." Occasionally I babysat her while Connie worked. I didn't like babysitting while Ricky was home because he never stopped drinking and had gotten worse.

While I was going through hardships because of my marriage to Ricky, my sister Nae went through a terrifying situation. This was the summer of 1984 in Sidney, Ohio. While her husband, Jon, was out, Nae was sitting on her front porch reading her Bible while swinging her three-year-old daughter, Jasmine. Jasmine was thirsty, so Nae left her on the swing to go inside for some water. From the time Nae stood up and started through her doorway, the Lord was telling her not to leave Jasmine alone. As soon as Nae stepped through her doorway, the Lord gave Nae a vision—Nae saw Jasmine in the back seat of a car, screaming, "Mommy." Nae was holding on to the door handle, trying to get it open as the driver was driving away. Then the vision left. Nae rushed back outside, grabbed Jasmine, and took her inside her home. Nae never left Jasmine alone again.

Later that summer, a neighbor lady who lived a few houses down from Nae told her that she had seen a car parked in a way that the driver could watch both houses. Every time Nae's neighbor opened the door of her home, the driver drove away. Nae felt in her heart that if she had left Jasmine on the porch alone that day, Jasmine would have been kidnapped. That has always been Nae's worst fear. Nae feels the Lord spared her and her daughter's lives through that vision that day. Because Nae obeyed the Lord, Jasmine grew into a beautiful lady with children of her own who fill our entire family's heart with joy.

CHAPTER 48

Ricky had a terrible temper. He cursed Daniel quite often and for no reason. I argued with him, trying to get him to stop, but he kept on. Ricky wouldn't allow Daniel to have many friends. I tried to reason with him, but he still wouldn't listen, so I let Daniel spend a lot of time with his adult friend Lee to keep Ricky from abusing him. Lee took Daniel fishing, hunting, and joyriding on four-wheelers, among other activities, and Daniel had a ball. My sister-in-law told me I wasn't being fair to Ricky because Ricky wasn't getting to spend much time with Daniel, but nevertheless I let Daniel go.

Ricky's family didn't know the extent of abuse that Daniel, Brianna, and I were going through. Ricky was jealous of Brianna, which caused him to argue more with me. Occasionally Ricky was pleasant, but then he would blow up unexpectedly. He turned abusive toward me, slapping, punching, pinching, cursing, and pulling my hair. I wore long sleeves in the hottest part of the summer to hide my bruised arms. Ricky became more hateful to me and Brianna as days went by.

One time, when Brianna saw his hatefulness toward me, she knocked his salad off the counter and onto the floor. I knew he was headed toward her to hit her. I was able to reach him before he could do her much harm. I grabbed the back of his shirt and ripped it as I pulled him backward away from her and then stepped between them. My mind then went blank. The next thing I heard was Daniel telling Ricky to leave me and Brianna alone, and then I saw Ricky push Daniel to the floor and kick him in the area of his fresh operation from a kidney removal. I tried stopping Ricky. Daniel finally escaped and ran out of our mobile home. Ricky put another shirt over his torn one and then left. Daniel stayed away for two days. When he came home, he, Brianna, and I talked about the incident. They said I slapped Ricky. I said that I didn't, but they insisted. I believed them and left it alone.

My brothers Micah and Kyle Anthony moved down from Kentucky and lived with Caleb and Babbie. Occasionally I stayed with them on weekends until Ricky was sober enough to work. Occasionally I stayed at Connie's or Aunt Elaina's. Then I thought of how unfair I was to burden them because of the mess I had gotten myself into. I tried staying home when Ricky went on his rampages. I tried going from room to room and even hiding between beds, but he found me. When he fell asleep, it was a major relief, but he would wake up still drunk and start all over again.

Then I bought mosquito wicks and went to my favorite park at night. I would watch the moon shine on the water as I sang and prayed until it was safe to go home.

I got a job at a local restaurant. I worked in the kitchen. Everything was taking a toll on me—trying to work, trying to keep my home clean and in order, worrying about the kids, trying to pay the bills, and dealing with Ricky's abusiveness. There were times when Ricky tried making up with me by bringing me flowers at my workplace. I threw them in the trash. Even though my marriages were all for the wrong reasons, I still tried to make them work. I also repented. Speaking of repentance, there's a song titled, "It's Me Again, Lord." I believe it would be safe to say I have been one of the hardest Christians with whom the Lord has ever dealt. I'm glad his grace and love surpass all understanding. There's no other word for grace but amazing!

I started going to a small church that was near a deep canal about two miles from my home. I had a wonderful pastor, Jeff Peters, and his wife, Beula. I confided in them about Ricky's and my problems. The Peters's gave me a key to the kitchen part of the church in case I needed a peaceful place to stay. I sneaked a pillow and a blanket into the kitchen and hid them.

The church became my hideaway home most of the time. The entire Peters family were such sweethearts; they stood by me through thick and thin. Their son and I were very close. He was special to me. The Peters never told others about my marriage problems. I tried hiding many of my problems from my family. Brianna and I would have to walk to our hideaway when Ricky would go into drunken rages. If I tried taking my pickup, Ricky would hear the motor and run out and stop me, so Brianna and I had to sneak quietly away. We even walked in the wintry rain, and we slept on the kitchen floor of the church. We didn't mind, it was peaceful. Occasionally Daniel went with us. After a particular church service was over, Ricky showed up. To keep from causing a scene, Brianna and I got in the car with him. While he was driving us home, he threatened to run us into the deep canal near the church.

I whispered to Brianna to hold on to the door handle;

if Ricky went toward the canal I told her to jump out and I would do the same. Just as he was heading for the canal and Brianna and I were about to open the door, he pulled back onto the road. Occasionally Ricky went to church with me. He was trying to straighten up his life, which made me feel good.

During one of our church services, Ricky finally went to the altar and got saved. He occasionally had our pastor, Reverend Jeff Peters, to come to our home to talk to him. Ricky was a new person, and I just knew we were going to see better days. But my heart was shattered when he started drinking again. Ricky asked me to go to an AA meeting, and I did, but that didn't last long. I rarely had any peaceful days when Ricky was home. I was getting to be a nervous wreck, almost to the point of completely losing my mind.

I was feeling extremely tired one evening and lay down to take a nap. When I awoke, I just stared at the ceiling, not knowing where I was or who I was. When my mind returned, I was frightened and thought about Grandma.

On another one of Ricky's drunks, when he came home, the kids and I were watching TV. No one said a word. Ricky came over to me and grabbed my arm. As I stood up, he twisted it behind my back, causing me to fall over the couch. Brianna and Daniel kept telling him to stop but he wouldn't. They were afraid to use our phone, so they threatened to go to the neighbors to call the law. Ricky said that if they called the law, I would be unrecognizable when they got back, so they didn't leave me. Then, being the cruel man that he was, he told them if they would say "please," he would let me go. When Ricky heard the word "please," he turned me loose.

Occasionally I saw the good side of Ricky. We went

fishing, we talked civil to each other, and even laughed and played around, which gave me fresh hope of things working out. In 1984, Brianna had grown up and had become pregnant with her first child. Brianna hadn't been pregnant long when I took her to her doctor's appointment. While she was in the examining room, the receptionist asked me what my name was. I told her "Alice", and then my mind went blank. I knew I had a last name but couldn't think of it. I knew I had a maiden name, but I couldn't think of it either. I just stood there with a puzzled look on my face. For a few seconds, I couldn't say anything, but then it finally came back to me, and I was able to tell her my full name.

Bo was in town and sent word for me to come to an old pool hall where we once often hung out. The owner was a good friend to me and Dad and my brothers Caleb and Micah. Tommy, among other friends of ours, stayed there until closing time, so I wasn't worried when I asked Brianna if she would go with me and go to the door and ask for Bo. She was of age to go in if she chose, but I told her not to. I believed if I went alone, I would be accused of cheating on Ricky. After getting to the pool hall, Brianna went in because she didn't know what Bo looked like and the noise drowned out her voice as she asked for him. Brianna and Bo walked out. Bo and I spoke for a little while, and he said he was divorced. He gave me a phone number and told me to call him the next day to meet at a nearby restaurant for coffee. I called but couldn't get in touch, so he went back to Alabama.

Ricky knew June had cheated on him, and maybe he didn't trust me either. Maybe that's why he had a bad attitude. I had tried to be the best I could to him. What hadn't I tried? In hopes that I could change Ricky's attitude, I decided to try something different. I fixed a nice candlelight dinner. The kids weren't going to be home that night, so I hoped everything would go well. Of course, he came home drunk. It broke my heart, but I still hoped for the best. He sat at the table and cried, saying what a good wife I was. He said that no one had ever done anything like that for him before. No sooner had he said that than he hit the table with his fist and cursed me. I got mad and knocked some food off the table. He started pulling my hair and made me pick it up. I got away, and he lay down and went to sleep.

In the spring of 1985, Brianna's daughter, Tonya, was born. Brianna got married, but it wasn't long before she got divorced. Amber, Connie's daughter, was still very tiny but no longer a baby in diapers. Connie was having troubles of her own and took Amber to Jellico to Mom's. She left her there until she could get back on her feet after she moved up there for a while with Amber, Marisol, and Cassandra. I wanted to get away from Ricky. I hated to leave Dad, but I believed he would be all right. He was living with us, and he and Ricky got along well. I had become tired in mind and body. So, I moved to Kentucky and lived with Mom and K. I helped Mom and K take care of Amber and her sisters. After a few months, Connie took Amber and her sisters back to Florida, and I thought about getting a divorce.

Mom and K had been going to a church in Tennessee with their pastor, Andy, and his wife, Bernice. One night while I was in church with mom and K, Bernice told me that Ricky had called her house saying that he was making plans to come up. Ricky had never liked to use the phone book, so I hid Andy and Bernice's phone number in the book in a place I thought Ricky would never look just in case he decided to use it. Well, he decided to look in the book and found Andy's phone number and made the call. I sure didn't want Ricky to come up there, so I went back to him in hopes he would change. When I got home, Ricky was so happy that we had gotten back together that he straightened up for a day. Well, at least I was queen for a day!

CHAPTER 49

While things remained the same between Ricky and me, Connie started working in a convenience store. Dad stayed with Connie and babysat her five-year-old daughter, Marisol, and two-year-old, Amber. Dad fell asleep and the girls found their way outside. While sitting on the steps of the trailer, Marisol decided that she wanted to see her mom. She asked Amber if she wanted to see Mommy too, and Amber said yes. Marisol took Amber's hand and started walking. They managed to cross a very busy and dangerous highway. It's a sheer miracle they weren't killed. There were many sugarcane trucks along with other large, heavy vehicles that traveled that highway. The first store they came to they thought was Connie's workplace. When the frightened little girls went in, the clerk asked them who they were looking for, and they said their mom. A police officer came in and started talking to the girls. About that time, Connie's girlfriend Andrea came into the store to buy some ice. When she saw the girls, she asked them if they were looking for their mom, and they said yes.

Andrea told the officer that she knew the children's mother and that she would take them to her. The officer let them go. Andrea brought the girls to Connie just about the same time Dad came in looking for Amber and Marisol. Dad felt bad about it and apologized to Connie several times. After Connie was told what happened, she became nervous to the point of getting sick to her stomach and was unable to continue her work. Her boss sent her home so that she could get herself settled down. Connie thanked the Lord for sparing her girls' lives!

CHAPTER 50

In the spring of 1987, Brianna had her second daughter, Cece. Then she met Don. Ricky talked about buying a boat, and he said that he wouldn't drink while fishing in it. That sounded great, so when Father's Day rolled around, I bought him one from Brianna's boyfriend, Don. It wasn't much to look at, but it was all I could afford. On our first fishing trip with the boat, Ricky took his beer along and started drinking. I was hurt and mad. We got into a verbal fight after we returned home.

One night when Ricky came home drunk, he started hitting me with his fist, and I pushed him over our dresser. The next day, I looked in the mirror and one side of my face was bruised. I went to my pastor's home and stayed there until my face healed. By 1988, Brianna had her third daughter, Marla.

My dad took ill with a mild case of tuberculosis and had to stay in the hospital. When his illness was under control, he was able to come home on weekends. We moved him into our home, so I could take care of him. Earlier I had asked Ricky to ask Dad if he would move in with us because I worried about his health and drinking. Occasionally, when I visited him in the past when he lived alone, he would get so drunk he would fall off his steps and couldn't get up, so I wanted to take care of him. I asked Dad to move in with us, but he wouldn't. I believed he would do it for Ricky. They got along well, so when Ricky asked, Dad moved in with us. Although Ricky didn't abuse me around Dad, believe it or not, that wasn't my purpose for wanting Dad to live with us!

Jane had sent word that she wanted to see me. I went to see what she wanted. She said she was moving to Michigan and asked me if I would keep her gun. I asked her, "Why don't you take it with you?" I told her I didn't want a gun in my home or around Ricky. She told me to hide it and took out the bullets, so I finally agreed to take it home. I hid it under some blankets in my bathroom closet. Neither Ricky nor Dad knew it was there.

Mom, K, Trey, and their friend Hailey came down from Kentucky to visit. After they left my home and went to see Connie, Ricky showed his anger because he was jealous. He didn't want me to have anything to do with anyone but his family and my dad. Ricky sat on our kitchen floor and tore the shirt he was wearing into shreds. Well, at least it wasn't me he tore!

Mom, K, Trey, Hailey, and I took Ricky's boat to the lake to go joyriding. After getting to the lake, Mom stayed on the shore while the rest of us went joyriding. We were pretty far away from shore when the motor quit. K and Trey tried to get it started, but it just wouldn't work. K, Trey, and I paddled with our hands, but we were getting nowhere. The wind was blowing pretty hard. Someone—me—got the bright idea for Trey to hold up his large yellow raincoat. Trey looked so funny, we all burst out laughing. K was watching the gators. Finally, some Good Samaritans came along and pulled us to shore. A few days later, my family and Hailey went back to Kentucky.

While Dad was home for the weekend, Ricky and I made plans to borrow Ricky's brother's camper to camp at the lake. We invited Dad, and he said he would come out later. After getting the camper set up, it was very late, so we called it a night. The next morning started with a good breakfast and then we went fishing. Ricky took his beer along. I was hurt, as usual, but I loved fishing and went anyway. He ran out of beer and headed to shore. The motor quit, and we used the trolling motor.

After getting to shore, I walked to our campsite while Ricky stayed and worked on the motor. When the rope broke, Ricky came to our campsite looking for his long yellow-handled screwdriver. Dad had come to our campsite in his van. When I saw Ricky drinking Dad's liquor, I purposed in my heart that I wasn't going out in the boat with Ricky. Ricky wasn't extremely mean when he drank a little beer, but when he mixed it with liquor, he was impossible to be with. While I was sitting in my lawn chair and Dad wasn't looking, Ricky hit my breast with the heavy handle part of the screwdriver and turned my chair over, causing me to fall out. Then he laughed.

When Ricky went back to fix the motor, I asked Dad if he would take me home and then to Connie's. He said okay, so we left. I intended to take some clothes and spend the rest of the weekend with her. After getting home, I changed my mind about taking my clothes. I was very tired of dragging them everywhere. As sweaty as I was, I rushed with my shower and changed clothes. As I started out of the bathroom, there stood Ricky in front of me, mad as a hornet, telling me, "You think you're cute, don't you?" Then he started slapping me and pulling my hair and tried to pull me out of the bathroom by my arm. I held on to the door while telling him I wasn't going back to the lake. He gave up, but what he said next made my blood turn cold. He said, "I will kill you like I did June," and then he left.

Dad was outside waiting for me. I took the gun from its hiding place, loaded it, and was going to put it in my purse and take it to Connie's for protection, just in case Ricky found me there. As I headed toward the living room where my purse was, Ricky came in with little Ricky. That caused me to freeze. I sure didn't want little Ricky to be in harm's way. I put the gun behind my back and warned Ricky that I had one, hoping he would leave me alone, sober up, and no one would get hurt. Little Ricky was crying extremely hard, begging his dad to leave also. Little Ricky had used the phone before, so I told him to dial 911, but all he could do was cry. Ricky tried kicking the gun out of my right hand. He grabbed my right arm and swung it in the air. I held on to the gun as tight as I could, hoping it wouldn't discharge. Somehow, we wrestled ourselves into the kitchen corner.

Hearing the commotion, Dad came in. He saw what was taking place and told Ricky to behave himself, but that didn't help. Ricky and I wrestled over to the kitchen sink. I yelled for Dad to call 911, but he just stood still. Ricky finally turned me loose. I was backing away from Ricky and bumped into Dad. Dad gently reached out and grabbed the gun from my hands. Ricky saw this and told Dad he was only playing. Dad and I were silent, then three shots rang out, and I started blacking out as Ricky was falling.

When everything became silent, I remembered pulling myself up from the counter. I saw Ricky on the floor and Dad standing in front of me with the gun pointed to his head. I begged him not to shoot himself and to give me the gun. When he gave it to me, I ran to dial 911, but I kept missing the numbers. I ran to my next-door neighbor's home and told her my husband had been shot and asked her to call for help. While the police were on their way, little Ricky, Dad, and I stood outside waiting for them to show up.

After the law came, Dad, little Ricky, and I were placed in separate cars and taken to the station, where we were questioned separately. This was in 1988. Dad was charged with first-degree murder. While Ricky was being buried, one of his brothers threatened my life in the presence of Mom and K, but we remained silent.

About a week later, while I was driving home from a neighboring town, a good feeling came into my heart, letting me know that Ricky was in heaven. Not long afterward, the feeling repeated itself. I believe he's up there. It doesn't take long for one to repent. It just takes a sincere heart.

After Dad went to court, he was charged with a lesser crime and spent a year behind bars. I was told there were strong reasons to believe Ricky had killed June, but there wasn't enough evidence to prove it.

In 1991, Caleb and Babbie moved close by; my brother Kyle moved to Mom and K's; Dad moved to another small town over from Caleb and Babbie; and I'm not for sure where Micah lived at the time. I know he ended up in Ohio. Dad occasionally walked across the bridge to a liquor store. I asked him not to, but he wouldn't listen. I worried that I would find him dead in the canal. We had made a lot of enemies in Ricky's family and friends.

Brianna and her boyfriend, Don, had a family of their

own. I bought Brianna a small trailer so that she could have a home of her own as well. It wasn't much, but she owned it and loved it. They moved to southwest Florida, and I visited them. Then they moved back to the eastern part of the state, where her doctor was. In the summer of 1991, they had their daughter Allie. Connie moved in with her ex-husband Jose in a small community near the center of Florida.

There were many bad memories in my hometown—the town I loved and called my home. It hurt me to move away, but I believed it was for the best. Before I moved, I asked Caleb to move Dad with him since he was planning to move Connie's way. Caleb agreed, and I moved to Connie's.

Caleb moved Dad to Connie's, then Caleb and Babbie bought a tent and moved to a campground close by. Caleb cut trees for the owner in exchange for food and rent for his tent. They were really roughing it! Berto, Vanessa, Violet, Marisol, and Amber played in the lake until Caleb spotted baby gators.

I wanted to spend the night at the camp. Night came, and I stretched out in my lawn chair and used a fan to keep the mosquitoes off me. I stayed awake most of the night watching for gators. I was ready to jump on top of Caleb's car if one happened to stroll my way, but my eyes started feeling heavier as the night went on, and I finally drifted off. When morning came, I checked myself, saying, "I'm alive."

CHAPTER 51

I moved to Mom and K's. Caleb and Babbie moved with their three kids to a town in central Ohio, just about a two-hour drive from where Micah, Nae, and her husband, Jon, lived. Meanwhile, in Florida, Connie and Jose separated. He and Cassandra moved to North Carolina. Cassandra ended up on the coast of North Carolina. Connie was brokenhearted and in a state of confusion. The Lord wanted her to return to him (the Lord), where she once was. I believe the Lord has people in different denominational churches, which is a good thing! There were three different denominational churches that Connie had to pass on her way to the post office. Every time she passed the Church of God, the Lord spoke to her, saying, "You need to go to church." This went on for about two months; she couldn't shake that feeling. Finally, one Sunday morning, Connie, Marisol, and Amber went to church. Connie could hardly wait until altar call. When it was given, she almost ran to it. She didn't wait to kneel but stood with her arms stretched toward heaven, repenting and asking for the Lord's forgiveness.

The Lord put her out in his spirit dancing. She didn't know she was in the world. When it was over, she knew the Lord blessed her in a very special way. It doesn't matter how we repent as long as we do and are willing to allow the Lord to use us the way he sees fit!

Connie called Mom to tell her, K, and me that she got saved. We were all so excited! Connie asked me if I would help her move to Mom and K's. I was more than glad to. Connie and I didn't stay at Mom's long. We moved to Ohio, where Dad had moved earlier near Micah, Nae, and Jon.

CHAPTER 52

Mom received an unexpected and exciting phone call. It was Stacy. She and Stephen asked Mia to help them locate their dad. Mia helped them. Arrangements were made for Stacy and Stephen to meet Caleb at Mom's house. The rest of us were called home.

There were tears of joy. My family and I have been to many reunions, but that one was the best. I have always liked Mia. We got along well together. I'm glad she made it easy for Stacy and Stephen to get in touch with their dad. Stephen moved to Caleb's, where Dad had moved earlier.

My brother Kyle Anthony was like Caleb and I used to be with drinking, stealing, and drugs. One night, while Mom, K, and I were in church, Kyle Anthony went with his friends to a party. Kyle Anthony was a bully, and he got into a fight with another bully named Tom, and Kyle Anthony humiliated him. When Tom went to his car, Kyle Anthony and his friends thought Tom was leaving, but he returned with a gun and shot Kyle Anthony three times.

Mom and K were informed about it while we were still in church. Mom got up from the pew but became too weak to move. She fell to the floor in shock and tears. Poor K tried to be strong for everyone, especially for Mom. K helped Mom up and into the car. Kyle Anthony was flown to a university children's hospital in Kentucky. Mom, K, and I, as well as other family members, rushed to be with him. His life was hanging in the balance. I believe with many prayers going up for him, the Lord spared his life and let him know how important it is to be saved.

After Kyle Anthony was discharged from the hospital, he met a girl named Dottie, and they started having problems in their relationship. Trey married Ruby, and they were blessed with a very precious son, Aiden. Aiden was born in the beginning of spring 1994. He had cerebral palsy, along with a heart defect. Trey and Ruby took Aiden to church with Mom and Kirby. While in church, Aiden would crawl to the altar and hold on to it to stand up and dance while laughing. We, as well as the church, held Aiden dear to our hearts. The congregation loved watching him. His favorite pastime was playing with a rocking chair while looking up toward heaven, laughing as though angels were playing with him.

Trey was a good husband. He was a very good father, and Ruby was a very good mother. Ruby and Trey started having problems in their relationship and ended up getting a divorce. Trey was awarded custody of Aiden. Mom and K took care of Aiden the most while Trey worked.

At this time, a lot was still going on in Kyle Anthony's life. Kyle Anthony and Dottie separated, and Kyle Anthony moved to Caleb and Babbie's home. Kyle Anthony and Dad thought the world of each other and got along well. They fixed themselves a place to live in Caleb's backyard. Caleb had a tree business of his own and hired Kyle Anthony to work for him. Kyle Anthony was a hard worker for Caleb and was straightening up his life. On one of Kyle Anthony's visits to Nae's home, he met a sweet girl named Paula. They were beginning to get serious about each other, and Kyle Anthony was straightening up his life even more. One night, after Dad and Kyle Anthony came home from shooting pool at the pool hall, Kyle Anthony wanted to visit Paula and asked Dad to go with him. Dad didn't feel well and told Kyle Anthony no. Kyle Anthony asked Stephen to go, but he also said no, so Kyle Anthony took off alone. He was driving over the speed limit and the law gave chase. Kyle Anthony threw his beer out of his car window while trying to outrun the law and slammed into a utility pole. While the ambulance was taking Kyle Anthony to the hospital, he passed away.

Kyle Anthony's childhood friend let Mom and K bury Kyle Anthony on his property where his own mom is buried. It was a blessing, because it is a very short walk from Mom and K's home. Thank you, Robby, for your compassion! This was in 1995. Soon after his death, Kyle Anthony's son from a previous relationship was born. He was named after his father. I call him Little Kyle. My sister Kat was given a picture of him. Kyle Anthony and his son could pass for twins. It took Mom a while before she was able to look at little Kyle's picture or visit with him because he reminded her so much of the son she lost, but she did love her grandson very much!

But now, although the heartbreak of Kyle Anthony's accident and his absence still lingers, Mom and K enjoy Little Kyle's visits. I know for a fact that sometime on his way to the hospital, Kyle Anthony repented, because shortly after he was buried, while I was standing in Mom's bathroom, the Lord showed me Kyle Anthony's wedding and birthday cake combined with large candles on top. I believe the Bible to be the complete truth. It speaks about the Christians going to a wedding in Revelation 19:9: "And he saith unto me, Write, blessed are they which are called unto the marriage supper of the Lamb. And he saith unto me, "these are the true sayings of God." Before one can go to the wedding supper, one must have a new birth. John 3:3 says, "Jesus answered and said unto him, Verily, verily, I say unto thee, Except a man be born again, he cannot see the kingdom of God." Not only did the Lord show me Kyle Anthony's wedding and birthday cake with large candles on top, he also showed me Kyle Anthony resting in heaven with a yellow glow around him, and the Lord literally allowed me to feel his peace. The Lord showed me all these things through a vision.

CHAPTER 53

Mom and K still live in the same place. I met a very sweet man in the town where my mom lived. It had been seven years that I had been alone, and it felt good to feel the warmth of a companion. We rode around quite a bit and talked; we also ate out. He was nice, friendly, and good to me.

In 1996, I started thinking of how good Bo used to be to me too. My mind went back to the year when he and I talked at that small pool hall, and he told me he was divorced. I wanted to get in touch with him. I felt Lizz would know where he was. I had wanted to get in touch with Lizz for a long time anyway, so I thought this would be a good time to do it. I located Lizz with the help of others and asked her about Bo. She gave me his address, so I wrote to him and sent him K's phone number. He called. We wrote and called often.

Brianna had moved to Tennessee some years earlier. Bo and I met at Brianna's home, then after a short visit, we returned to our own homes. We continued meeting at Brianna's a little longer because it saved Bo some driving time and made it easier on him because of the long hours he had to work.

He asked me to come to his home in north-central Alabama and stay a little while so we could get better reacquainted. I stayed a few months. In the spring of 1996, Bo and I got married, and our love for each other grew.

Dad had been diagnosed with cancer while he was living with Caleb and Babbie in Ohio. Then in 1997, I felt strongly that I wanted to help out, so I called Caleb and asked him to ask Dad if he would move to Alabama so that I could take care of him. Dad said yes. Babbie drove Dad down to Alabama to be with me. It was at this point that I decided to force myself to call him "Daddy" again. It felt so good to be able to refer to him as my daddy again so long after being shamed for calling him that to begin with. She said it broke her heart to drive away from him. She had helped Caleb take care of him for a long time. Soon afterward, Caleb and Babbie moved to a place near me. Connie also moved down and stayed with me. We helped one another take care of Daddy. As cancer took its toll on Daddy, it was very heartbreaking to see our strong, healthy dad who used to take care of us become a bedfast skeleton and suffer so much.

Nae and Micah were called down to see him. We all gathered at his bedside and one by one gave him a kiss, letting him know we were there for him. I'm glad he knew who we were, and he responded to us.

Daddy never cared about TV preachers, but when he saw one popular televangelist, he really enjoyed watching him. When Daddy let us know he made things right with the Lord, we were relieved and at peace. When he passed away, it was bittersweet. Bitter because it hurt to see him go, and sweet because he was no longer in pain. And to me, it was an honor for him to meet the Lord from my home that year of 1997.

Daddy was laid to rest on a warm summer afternoon. Before Caleb moved down to be with Daddy, Caleb went to church. The Lord spoke to him through prophecy, telling

Spared

him that if he gave his heart to him (the Lord), he would save his family. Not long after Caleb got saved, the Lord saved his family. The Lord always holds to his word.

Now Caleb helps us pray and the Lord answers, like this next incident. After Daddy was taken to the morgue, Connie, Caleb, and I were standing in my kitchen. We were in total silence, when all of a sudden, the Lord gave me a vision: the Lord was holding Daddy in his arms. Daddy was shown to me as a little lamb. When the Lord set him down in heaven, Daddy became a full-grown sheep. As Daddy trotted further up into heaven, he went to a small group of sheep that the Lord showed to me to be his blood family. They were grazing while waiting for Daddy to join them. Just as soon as Daddy reached them, they all trotted further up into heaven. The further they trotted upward, the bluer heaven became. I felt such awesome peace. Then the vision left.

As soon as I told Connie and Caleb the vision, Caleb said he had been praying that if Daddy had made it to heaven, the Lord would show one of us. He didn't care who. I know the devil tries to put doubt in our minds, but when the Lord reveals himself, it gives extra strength to fight the devil.

I love to listen to Caleb speak about the Lord. He studies the Bible, prays, and fasts, and the Lord gives him knowledge. He loves spreading the gospel. He and Babbie enjoy serving the Lord.

Mom developed health problems. I wanted to move close to her to be with her, and Bo moved with me. He had never been away from his kids, so after a while he moved back to Alabama. I was hurt at first, but I understood, and I eventually moved back also. Ever since I became a Christian, I have met some very precious friends in different denominational churches, and friends who don't go to church as well.

CHAPTER 54

By the beginning of fall in 1999, Trey and Aiden had been staying with Mom and K for a while. To keep Aiden from falling out of bed and getting hurt, Mom and K had made Aiden a bed on the floor with his favorite blanket on K's side of the bed. One morning, Aiden reached up and started rubbing K's head and laughing. Suddenly, while K was playing with him, Aiden had a massive seizure. Mom and K rushed him to the hospital. He was then transported to a university children's hospital in Tennessee, where he passed away. His passing was very heartbreaking and hard to bear. Mom and K were close friends with the gospel group who sang at Aiden's funeral. Aiden was laid to rest beside his uncle Kyle Anthony.

A few years after Aiden's passing, in 2001, Bo took me to Florida to visit Lizz. I had wanted to see her for a long time. Just to hear her voice when I had called her to ask about Bo's whereabouts was exciting. She and her husband had been Christians now for a long time, and we went to church together. What a major change for us. Speaking of church, I had made many mistakes in and out of church, but the Lord finally got my attention through his chastisement, and I'm so glad!

Trey married a woman named Patricia. It was a blessing

for them to have each other. She is a ray of sunshine in all our lives. It seemed to be love at first sight, and it was a dream come true for Trey when Patricia came into his life. Another dream came true for Trey, as well as for K, when they had the privilege to go to Colorado for an elk hunting trip. It was a twenty-five-hour drive, but it would turn out to be worth it.

Once they arrived at their camp in Colorado, they met up with Patricia's dad and uncle. After getting settled in, they rested up for the following day, which was opening day for elk hunting. They got up a few hours before daylight for a hearty breakfast. After leaving their cabin by 10:00 a.m., Trey killed his first bull elk, a four-by-four pointer. He was so excited he could hardly get out of his tree stand. K had to sadly go back to the camp empty-handed. Trey felt sorry for his dad and prayed for the Lord to bless him with an elk.

A few days later, they headed back to their tree stands for another long day of bitter cold. Then K saw his elk. With hearts pounding, they waited. Out from the brush it came. K took a deep breath, shouted, "Bless the Lord, I see it!" and then he shot and hit his mark. After locating it, it was a beautiful five-by-five elk. After field dressing it and getting it back to camp, it was K's turn to tell the story of the elk that didn't get away. These beautiful trophies hang on their walls to this day as a reminder of their adventurous trip to the Colorado mountains.

CHAPTER 55

    This is a terrifying incident concerning my cousin Denny and his wife, Claire, who moved to Tennessee from Florida. They not only had their son, but they had a daughter also. Their kids are now grown. Denny and Claire had just returned from town and were about to get out of their car to go inside their two-bedroom, two-bath mobile home. Denny told Claire to stay in the car because he didn't like the way the weather was looking. Their daughter and her girlfriend were in their pickup truck, listening to the news. She was still a good distance from her parents' home, so she speeded out to warn her parents that a tornado was headed their way.

    As she slid sideways into her parents' yard, the wind started blowing with such force that it took all of Denny's strength to rush to her and pull her out of her truck and force her into his car, then also do the same with her girlfriend. Claire and Denny laid on top of the girls in the floorboard. With voices screaming as the tornado tried sucking them out of the car, it was total terror. Denny prayed, "Lord, if anyone has to die, please let it be me and let my family live." The tornado picked up the car and held it in midair; it may have been a couple of seconds, but to them it felt much longer. After the car was set back down, the tornado picked up Denny and

Claire's mobile home, and it exploded in midair. Contents came crashing down on top of the car.

With all that was going on, Claire still managed to hold on to her flashlight, and Denny held on to his cell phone—the very things they needed to call for help in all the darkness that covered them. When help arrived, they had to cut mangled wires and power lines among other debris away from the car. Denny and the others were finally freed and taken to the hospital, where they were checked out and found uninjured.

CHAPTER 56

Another terrifying incident occurred concerning my sister Connie's daughter, Cassandra, her boyfriend, Jacob, and their friend who they called "Boss" while they were living in Shallotte, North Carolina. In the spring of 2002, Cassandra woke up one morning to run her mail route. It was the same old routine. Nothing felt different that day than any other day. She got ready for work, hopped into her truck, and left. The mail was light that day, and it didn't take her long to get it done. She started thinking about her second job at the restaurant.

Jacob, a new man in her life who was a breath of fresh air and with whom she had fallen deeply in love, also worked at the restaurant. Jacob shared his home with their friend Boss. Boss had a couple of friends named Boogie and Morton. Boogie and Morton went to a strip club and met a stripper named Tammy. She was in a partnership with two criminals. Tammy persuaded Boogie and Morton to have a private strip party with her. Boogie and Morton arranged with Boss to have the party at his place. After they got to Boss and Jacob's home, Boogie and Morton asked Boss if he wanted to watch Tammy perform. Boss told them he had some plumbing work to do, but that he would take a peek later and left the room.

At the restaurant, Cassandra and Jacob were worn out and cranky and ready to get out of there. It had been a long week for them both. Cassandra asked Jacob if he wanted to spend the night with her. Surprisingly, he said no, so she dropped him off at his home. When she saw that Boss had company, it caused her to get even more upset. Harsh words were exchanged between them, and then she went home. By 10:00 p.m., the party at Boss and Jacob's was ending. Boogie and Morton took Tammy back to the club. Tammy told her two criminal partners that Boss had money in his home. Around that time, Cassandra got to feeling bad about the way she had acted and the things she had said to Jacob. She showered, changed her clothes, and went to Jacob's home. Cassandra didn't see Boss. She thought he wasn't home, but he was in his bedroom asleep. She didn't ask about Boss's whereabouts because she had her mind focused on apologizing to Jacob. After Cassandra and Jacob had apologized to each other, it was late, and they went to bed.

That next morning, around 7:30 a.m., Jacob and Cassandra were awakened by a rapid knocking on the door. When Jacob answered it, it was Tammy's two criminal partners. They forced their way into the home. One had a gun and pointed it at Jacob and ordered him to get on the floor.

The gunman asked Jacob if anyone else was in there. Jacob said it was just him and Boss. The noise woke up Boss and he staggered to the living room entrance. The gunman grabbed Boss, and he went to the floor. The criminals were yelling, "Where's the money?" Boss and Jacob told them that they didn't have any money. The gunman shot Boss in his leg—Boss tried to escape but was shot in his leg again.

Jacob started praying. Cassandra woke up. She realized

they were being robbed. More shots rang out, seven in all. Boss told Jacob that he was dying and to tell his mother he loved her. Hearing all that was going on, Cassandra got up and hid in the bedroom closet. The criminals found some gas and poured it on Jacob and Boss and all over the living room When Cassandra heard the criminals talking about a lighter, she quietly opened the door and grabbed the lighter from off the dresser.

Before she could shut the door, in walked the gunman and caught her. He took the lighter from her hand. She raised her hands up and closed her eyes. Then, with a voice that chilled her soul, he told her to get on the bed and not move. She did as she was told. The gunman grabbed a blanket and returned to Jacob and Boss.

Cassandra knew the only way to get to heaven was through repentance of one's sins, so she prayed. Suddenly she felt such awesome peace, knowing the Lord had forgiven her. The criminals set the living room on fire and told Jacob if he got up, he would get shot. Then the criminals left. Jacob knew he couldn't just lay there, so he jumped up and ran to rescue Cassandra. Jacob told her that Boss was dead, but then they heard Boss say, "I'm not dead yet." Jacob and Cassandra knew they had to save Boss. Cassandra ran to her automobile, and she and Jacob rushed Boss to the hospital. Although Boss is now paralyzed from the incident, he, Jacob, and Cassandra thank the Lord for sparing their lives that terrifying day. The criminals were caught after being aired on *America's Most Wanted*. Thanks! Cassandra and Jacob have since gotten married and now have a beautiful daughter named Kaitlyn.

CHAPTER 57

In 2005, on another trip to see Lizz, Bo and I were able to visit Anne with Lizz's help. I had wanted to get in touch with Anne for a long time. I had her mom's phone number but couldn't find it. With Lizz's help, I called Anne, and we arranged to visit her at her home in Florida. I had the pleasure of meeting her husband, and he was a great host to Bo and me.

It was also a special treat to visit Lida. We had all married around the same time. My daughter, Brianna, had enjoyed playing with Lida's children. Lida, Lizz, Anne, and I gave Anne's mom a surprise visit. I felt like singing "Hail, Hail, the Gang's All Here." That was a very special gathering, and I hope to be able to do it again. Since Lizz, her husband, Anne, and I have become Christians, we can band together with our prayers for others; what a joy!

CHAPTER 58

Brianna's Stories

My name is Brianna, but my family calls me Brie. I was born in the fall of 1967 in south Florida at 4:22 a.m.

As a young girl, there were things that happened to me that no child should have to go through. I was six years old when my mom, Alice, and dad, Landon, divorced. Mom and I went through good and bad times during Mom and Dad's marriage and after their divorce. I was six-and-a-half years old when my worst abuse began, so in total to me I have been abused to the max.

My dad's dad is my Grandpa Lou, who married Joni, and they had three children: John, Rodney, and Suzanne. Joni was a good cook. I liked everything she cooked except tomatoes. I would leave them on my plate, but she made me eat them.

I tried so hard to swallow them, but they just wouldn't stay down. They made me sick. Joni told me if I threw them up, I would have to clean them up. Well, I threw them up and had to clean them up, and then she put more on my plate. I had to sit at the table for hours, because I refused to eat those nasty things. Finally, when she saw that I wasn't going to eat them, she let me get up. I wanted to play, but I had to help with the dishes, take my bath, and then go to bed. Mom taught me to respect my elders, and I tried.

Aunt Suzanne was mentally handicapped. I spent weekends with Grandpa Lou so I could play with Suzanne. Occasionally Joni made me help my uncles John and Rodney pick up cans. They took me under a store that stood on pilings. They touched my privates and made me do the same to them.

I had to help Joni roll newspapers and load them in her car for the next morning Three o'clock rolled around early for a little child, but I had no choice; I had to deliver papers. Joni assured Mom that I got plenty of sleep, so Mom never complained.

Joni and Grandpa took Suzanne, John, Rodney, and me skating. Suzanne and I didn't know how to skate. We held on to the bars and wall. I wanted to stay with Suzanne, but Joni made me get in the middle of the rink. I tried to follow the other kids, but they either ran over me or pushed me down. It bruised me up quite a bit. When Grandpa took me to Mom, he accused her of letting her boyfriend's bruise me. Mom fussed back, denying it. Mom must have thought that I got them from playing around. Mom did a lot of wrong things, but she never let anyone beat on me.

CHAPTER 59

Another sleepover, when I had to help my uncles pick up cans, they sexually abused me again. When I cried, begging them to stop, they hurt me more. They said if I told Mom, they would kill us both. When I went to Mom's, I kept silent and went outside and played. I loved it when Mom and I painted pictures and went for walks. Dad introduced me to his pretty girlfriend, Karen. I visited them on Fridays and played with Karen two youngest siblings. Karen and Dad got married.

Karen made grilled cheese sandwiches and tomato soup. I refused to eat them and threw them on the floor. When she cried, I felt sorry for her and told her I didn't like tomatoes, so she made chicken noodle soup. I was never mean to her anymore. The summer after Mom and Dad's divorce, Mom let me spend it with Dad. He agreed to bring me back to Mom when school started back in Florida. Dad took me to Texas where he and Karen lived.

When school started back, instead of Dad taking me to Mom's, he took me to Georgia to live with his mom, Marie, and stepdad, Tim—My Granny Marie and my Granddaddy Tim. They were long-distance truck drivers. Granddaddy drank a lot and was losing his eyesight. The company let him go. Mom thought I was with Dad.

Granny enrolled me in school. The school took my class on a trip. I won the crab race and received a blue ribbon and took it home to show Granddaddy. He was proud of me and fixed us a steak supper.

After I washed dishes, did my homework, and took my bath, Granddaddy asked me to bring him the Vaseline. When I did, he told me to get on the bed. I obeyed, and he put my hand on his privates and made me do the same to him. I cried. The next day, he told me to come straight home from school because we were going to Texas. Granddaddy sexually abused me several more times.

After getting to Dad's, I was relieved and very happy. I never wanted to go back to Granddaddy's. When it was time to go back to Granddaddy, I cried. When Karen and I were alone, she said I could tell her anything and she would keep it a secret if I wanted her to. I told her everything. She said that I didn't have to go with Granddaddy. They all got into an argument and then I was allowed to stay with Dad. While I was watching TV, I told Dad what Granddaddy had done to me, but he said he didn't want to hear it, so I kept silent once again.

I grew closer to Karen. She walked me to and from school across from our home to keep me safe. She cut my hair and showed me how to keep it fixed. She pierced my ears. I asked if I could call her "Mom," and she said that it was my choice but that she would be proud to have a brave daughter like me.

The next day while I was in class, Mom came in and grabbed my arm and wouldn't let go. I can't explain the joy I felt. I was ready to go home with her. When my teacher saw Mom holding my arm, she came to my rescue. Mom explained to her what Dad had done, and my teacher called the principal. Mom repeated her story to him, but he wasn't allowed to let me leave with Mom.

He told Mom she needed to take the situation to court. Mom got a lawyer, and he let Mom place me in a children's facility. I was scared and didn't know how long I would have to stay. Karen found out where I was and came to see me. When Mom saw Karen kiss me, they became friends. The judge gave me to Mom, and we went home.

Mom had a habit of being in and out of church. Most every time she quit going to church, she would drink. Soon after we came home from Texas, she quit going to church and started drinking again. She had been working on a sod farm but quit and started working in a packinghouse. I had to stay with my grandpa Lou again. He didn't know the abuse I was going through at the time. He worked while his family kept quiet. Joni went to the store, and once again John and Rodney started abusing me. This time the abuse was worse than ever. I ran into the bathroom and locked the door. I wanted to stay in there until Grandpa Lou came home, but I remembered I had to do dishes or Joni would whip me.

When I went to the kitchen, John said, "You got what you deserved," and then he threatened Mom's and my life again if I told. When Joni came home from the store, Suzanne told her what the boys had done to me.

Joni understood Suzanne, but she pretended not to. When Joni took me to Mom's, before I got out of the car, she said, "You better not say anything to your mom. If you do, I will beat you black and blue." When she said that, I knew she had understood Suzanne. I was one frightened little girl, so I never said a word.

Around 1977, Joni and John had a sharp argument. John

beat her black and blue. Mom and I were living with Mom's girlfriend. When Joni saw Mom's girlfriend Kay, she told Kay to tell Mom about the rape. When Kay told Mom, Mom was shocked. These were some of the very people she trusted, and so did I at first. Mom had been getting depressed and drinking more than ever and started dressing very trashy. After Kay told Mom what John had done to me, she and Kay stormed out with me and went to Joni's home. After Mom and Joni talked, Joni followed us to the police station. Mom reported the rape as Joni had told her. Joni admitted to the officers that it was true.

Mom threatened to kill John. After she calmed down, the officers took me in a room alone and questioned me. I couldn't speak well due to loss of hearing from having meningitis, so it was hard for me to explain the whole matter. Mom had taught me not to say bad words. However, she did say I could use them if anyone tried to harm me in anyway, but I still wouldn't say them. So, it was even harder for me when I tried to tell what John had done. I couldn't say my words right. I tried using substitute words, but that didn't help either. The officers laughed at me.

Joni's face was bruised, and she told the officers that her son, John, beat her up. The officers must have thought she made up the rape story for revenge. Mom was dressed very trashy, but that ended up being a very short-term phase. Mom felt that because of the way she was dressed, along with Joni's statement concerning her son beating her up and me not being able to explain the situation to their satisfaction, the officers didn't help her at all. So, Mom took it to court. But that was a waste of time also, she was told she had waited too long to report it, that it couldn't be proven, and Mom should just keep me away from them. That was something that woke Mom up about the way she was dressing, because it partially led to us not being taken seriously. After that, Mom stopped dressing trashy.

Mom's brother Caleb had a tough reputation. I don't know who told him about the rape, but when he saw John at a gas station in town and asked him about it, John laughed, not knowing who he was talking to (Joni's family my Mom's family never associated). So, John didn't know what Uncle Caleb looked like, but John was pointed out to Uncle Caleb, so Uncle Caleb beat John up, giving him a concussion and a broken jaw with just one punch.

Uncle Caleb's friend Guy told Uncle Caleb to run before the law got there, so he did. While John was in the hospital, he found out that Uncle Caleb was the one who put him there. When John was asked if he wanted to press charges, he said no.

Later on, in 1982, I was raped again by my mom's husband, Stewart. He also threatened my life and my mother's, saying that if I told anything, we'd both lose our lives. It wasn't long before they were divorced, but I didn't my mom about what happened until eleven years later, after I had all my children.

CHAPTER 60

When I was a young teen, Mom married Ricky, who used to be married to her girlfriend June. June had passed away. I hated Ricky with a passion. He was always accusing me of things I didn't do, so I stayed away as much as possible. I dated Allen, and we made plans to run away to Mississippi. We were leaving on a Wednesday night. Mom had started back to church when I was about twelve years old, and she made me go with her. Why I thought I could get out of going to church on a church night I don't know. But after I came home from church, some of my friends came over and told me that Alex had left. I cried.

I felt Mom didn't take up for me as much as she should have when I was accused of things I didn't do. She had focused her attention on Ricky's adopted son, Daniel, my stepbrother, because of the abuse he had to take from Ricky. This caused her to lose sight of my feelings. She loved Ricky's biological son, whom she called Little Ricky, but because of the different circumstances between the boys, she leaned more toward Daniel. Anyway, I was being treated unfairly, so I wanted to leave.

Mom occasionally allowed my girlfriend Zoe to spend nights with me. She was completely deaf. On one sleepover, we sneaked out of my bedroom window and ran away. A truck driver picked us up and took us to a town on the other side of the state. Zoe and I spent the night in a motel. Then I called Granny Marie and Granddaddy Tim, who lived in Tennessee. I just didn't know what else to do. Granny came and got me and sent Zoe back to her hometown. It was two days before Mom found out where I was. The police had an all-points bulletin out on me. When Granddaddy called her and talked to her on the phone, he told Mom he had waited that long to tell her where I was because she had been married too many times. He didn't explain that statement. He just left it alone.

When Mom and I spoke on the phone, she said all she could see in her mind was me being found dead somewhere in a ditch. She was terrified. She said I could stay with Granny and Granddaddy if I wanted to and come home when I was ready. She wasn't going to have me brought back to what I had run away from. At that time, she had no idea about the sexual abuse that had I suffered at Granddaddy's hands. Dad came and took me back to Texas. Even though I wasn't old enough, he gave me permission to drink and smoke pot.

I met William, who lived in the upstairs apartment above us. We drank and smoked pot together. One thing led to another, and I got pregnant. I never told a soul. not even William. Dad came home one night, and he and Karen got into an argument and separated. He told me I had to go with him. I asked if I could stay with Karen. He stood speechless. In the past he had accused me of trying to break them up, so I guess he was speechless when I chose her over him. He used my mom as an excuse to get me to go with him, saying she was sick and needed me. Dad knew that Karen knew he was going to Granddaddy's, and she would take Dad back just to keep me from staying alone with Granddaddy. He believed Karen loved me enough to keep me away from Granddaddy and it worked. Karen went back to him. Shortly afterward, I went back to Mom's.

CHAPTER 61

I worked in a packinghouse with Mom. I paid for my own doctor bills and necessities and gave Mom some money to help with the utilities. What was left, I put in my piggy bank. While I was in the hospital having my first child, Mom was with me. Ricky showed up drunk and tried to make Mom leave, but she refused. Mom was extremely hurt because she had spent two weeks in a Miami hospital with Ricky's son Daniel when he had a kidney removed, and Ricky didn't want Mom to spend one night with me. Ricky was so unfair, but I promised Mom I wouldn't run away again. In the spring of 1985, I had my daughter Tonya.

CHAPTER 62

Alex came back into my life, and we dated once more.
I got pregnant again. Things didn't work out, and we broke
up for good. A few months later, I had my second daughter,
Cecilia, who some family calls Cece. Then I met Don. We lived
together, and I got pregnant again. I had a rough pregnancy.
I was hoping everything would be all right and thank God it
was. Our daughter Marla was born in 1988.

Don moved us to another part of Florida, close to a
swamp. We occasionally camped behind our trailer and went
buggy riding. When Mom came to visit and walked to the
nearby store, she threw small rocks at the gators just to watch
their reactions. She never tried to hurt them; she just has
always been fascinated with them.

Don brought home a baby wild pig. We just about had it
raised when it went missing. Mom had been worried that it
would hurt one of us, so I thought she secretly did away with
it. It took me a long time before I got up the nerve to ask her
about it, because I didn't want to accuse her of stealing. When
I finally did, she laughed and said no. But she believes the
Lord answered her prayer when she prayed for it to run away. I
went to work in a tomato factory, of all places—imagine that!

I got pregnant with my fourth child, and I had to quit

my job because it made me too sick. When I was five months pregnant, it got to the point that I could hardly walk. I had the hardest pregnancy ever. It scared me, and I wanted to move back my hometown so that I could be closer to my doctor. Don moved us back. Our daughter Allie was born in the summer of 1991. All my girls were delivered by the same doctor. He was good, kind, and caring, and he believed in prayer. While Mom and I were in her backyard, I told her that I was going to have a baby boy even if it killed me. When Mom heard me say that, her face turned white. She got sick to her stomach and in a trembling voice she told me about how her Aunt Velma had made that same statement. That scared me, and I didn't try to have another child.

Don got into lots of fights with guys and made many enemies. He let his best friend drive his Ford Ranger pickup. When some guys saw him, they thought he was Don. They beat him nearly to death and threw him in a cane field, leaving him for dead. Don felt bad about it and was glad when his friend recovered. Shortly afterward, Don's mom and dad talked him into moving to Tennessee because they feared for his life. So, Don and I took our girls and moved there, where we have been ever since. Don's parents moved there also, and we live near one another.

On one of our visits to see Granddaddy Tim and Granny Marie in another part of Tennessee, Granddaddy Tim apologized for sexually abusing me. It was a step in the right direction. I forgave him, although he left painful scars in my heart. Not long afterward, he passed away. I'm thankful that Don is my husband. He has stood by me through thick and thin, ready to do whatever it takes to protect me and our girls.

Grandpa Lou and his family also lived close to Granny

and Granddaddy. Not long before Grandpa Lou passed away, he wanted to see me, but I refused because John and Rodney were there. I often wonder if Grandpa Lou wanted to apologize to me for what his sons and Joni had done to me.

CHAPTER 63

It is hard for me to cope with life's pressures because of my severe migraines and bad nerves from having meningitis. It doesn't take much for things to shake me up, but this next incident tore my nerves all to pieces. My girls were very young. A young man tried to get my girls to go horseback riding in the woods, but I refused to let them go. He was later caught with a little black book in his possession. In that little black book was a list of girls' names, including my girls'.

It just goes to show that there are a lot of sick and cruel people in this world. My heart goes out to all the poor abused children and abused adults as well.

May God Bless!